AF435021

Judges

50 Biblical Insights by **Gary Inrig**

Journey Through Judges
© 2015 by Gary Inrig
Published by Discovery House Publishing Singapore Pte. Ltd.
All rights reserved.

Discovery House Publishing™ is affiliated
with Our Daily Bread Ministries Asia Ltd.

Requests for permission to quote
from this book should be directed to:

Permissions Department
Our Daily Bread Publishing
P. O. Box 3566
Grand Rapids, MI 49501, USA

Or contact us by email at
permissionsdept@odb.org

Scripture taken from the Holy Bible, New International Version® Anglicized, NIV®
Copyright © 1973, 1978, 1984, 2011 by Biblica, Inc.® Used by permission.
All rights reserved worldwide.

This Discovery House edition is adapted from *Hearts of Iron, Feet of Clay: Practical
and Contemporary Lessons from the Book of Judges* by Gary Inrig. Copyight ©
1979, 2005 by Gary Inrig. Used by permission of Discovery House Publishing™.
All rights reserved.

Design by Joshua Tan
Typeset by Grace Goh

ISBN 978-981-11-7259-5

Foreword

We live in a time of immense moral and spiritual change, when massive
forces are pounding our culture. How do we live in a society that has no fixed
standards and is becoming more secular and pluralistic daily? When everyone
around us is doing what seems right in their own eyes, how do Christ-
followers keep on track, doing what is right in their Lord's eyes?

Some of the most relevant parallels to our modern situation can be found
in the book of Judges. It describes a time of moral, spiritual, and ethical
anarchy, a society without standards. Yet the Israelites living at that time were
very much like us—people with God-given potential for greatness but also
unfailing capacity for disaster. When they dared to trust God and depend
upon Him, they became people with hearts of iron, who made a positive,
godly impact on their times. But when even their greatest heroes depended
upon the flesh, they were revealed as people with feet of clay, who not only
experienced personal failure but also caused spiritual catastrophe.

As we study their lives and discover the great principles God reveals about
the way He works in—and often despite—His people, we can learn what it is
to live powerful, productive lives in the midst of a society that is increasingly
hostile to loyal followers of the One who alone is Lord.

All Glory to Him,
Gary Inrig

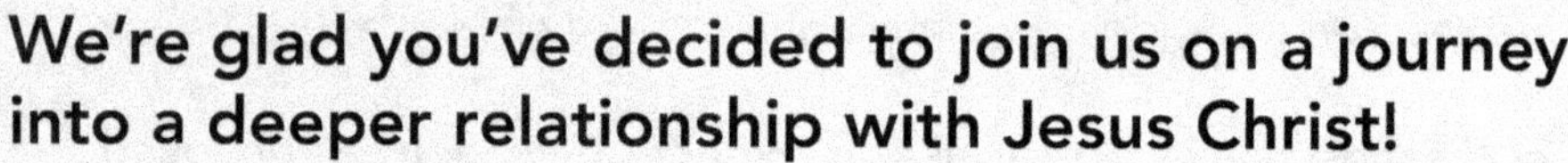

We're glad you've decided to join us on a journey into a deeper relationship with Jesus Christ!

The *Journey Through* series is designed to help believers spend time with God in His Word, book by book. Each title is written by a faithful Bible teacher to help you read, reflect, and apply God's Word, a little bit at a time. It's a great accompaniment to be read alongside the Bible, as you dig deeper into God's Word. We trust the meditation on God's Word will draw you into a closer relationship with Him through our Lord and Saviour, Jesus Christ.

How to use this resource

READ: After reading and reflecting on the Bible verses, use the explanatory notes to help you understand the Scriptures in fresh ways.

REFLECT: Use the questions to consider how you could respond to God and His Word, letting Him change you from the inside out.

RECORD: Jot down your thoughts and responses in the space provided to keep a diary of your journey with the Lord.

An Overview

The book of Judges is a long, sad story of defeat. It tells the story of unbelief
and disobedience, of a people increasingly divided; sliding into anarchy as
every person "did as they saw fit" (Judges 21:25). The theme of Judges is the
assimilation of God's people, Israel, by the pagan cultures that surrounded
them. Because these pagan people were broadly referred to as the
Canaanites, we can speak of the "Canaanisation" of Israel, which eventually
resulted in the Israelites losing all of their uniqueness as God's nation, making
them virtually indistinguishable from the surrounding peoples.

We are not told who wrote this book. Jewish tradition suggests that it was
Samuel, but his authorship cannot be proven.

Judges is a book that speaks to our time because it presents us with living
examples of people who were called to serve God in the midst of great
challenges, many of which were similar to those we face today. Sadly,
only a few of them provide us with positive examples. But there is a great
deal to be learned, not only from those who endured but also from those
who capitulated to the pressures and spirit of their age. Judges vividly
demonstrates to us the consequences of the spiritual compromise and
disobedience that arises when the world succeeds in squeezing believers into
its mould.

The Structure of Judges

1:1–3:6	Israel's assimilation: On the path of compromise
3:7–16:31	Israel's downward spiral, and God's judgment and discipline
17:1–21:25	Israel's fall into total depravity

Day 1

Read Judges 1:1–2

The opening words of Judges may at first glance seem to be only a helpful historical notation. Sadly, as we shall see, they represent the spiritual high-water mark of the entire book. The first phrase, "after the death of Joshua" (Judges 1:1), marks the beginning of a drastic decline in the spiritual well-being of the nation. **This decline was totally unnecessary, since Israel's wellbeing was not dependent on the greatness of its leaders but on the goodness of her God**.

Two verses indicate the vast difference between the time of Joshua and the period of the judges. As Joshua was about to die, he issued one last stirring challenge: "Choose for yourselves this day whom you will serve . . . But as for me and my household, we will serve the LORD." The people's response was instantaneous: "Far be it from us to forsake the LORD to serve other gods!" (Joshua 24:15–16). Early in the period of the judges, however, we have this verdict pronounced on the people: "The Israelites did evil in the eyes of the LORD; they forgot the LORD their God, and served the Baals and the Asherahs" (Judges 3:7). So in a few short years, "we will not forget the LORD" has become "the people forgot the LORD".

Why did that happen? How did a people who had known continuous victory by faith sink to become a nation experiencing constant failure due to compromise? And how can we guard against the same thing happening in our lives?

The death of Joshua marked a national crisis. The great leader had gone, and God had not elevated another leader to take his place. But the people, no doubt reflecting the godly influence of Joshua's life, respond with faith and trust. They gather together as a united people to seek God's direction and to carry out His mission (v. 1). First, they accept the Lord's authority. They don't just set out to do what seems best; they seek His direction. Second, they accept His mission—to take the land and exterminate the Canaanites. Third, they wait for the Lord's orders.

The Lord's choice of the tribe of Judah (v. 2) to take the lead is consistent with His plan to choose a king from Judah, a preview of the great day when His Messiah would be born as a descendant of David. But what should be noted here is the Lord's promise of victory: "I have given the land into their hands" (v. 2) This is the way it should be for God's people, but sadly, as we shall

see, they will never attain such heights again in
this book.

ThinkThrough

Is there a "high-
water mark" of
spiritual growth in
your life? How can
you go even higher?

How can you keep
your promise to
the Lord not to
forget Him?

Day 2

This passage seems to be a long list of ancient battles in distant places, with no possible relevance to our lives some 30 centuries later. However, a closer look suggests a pattern that is all too familiar, one we must carefully guard ourselves against.

The description of Israel's conquest begins in the southern region and traces Judah's campaign, which is much more successful than those of the other tribes—in the upland campaign around Jerusalem (vv. 4–8); the capture of the Hebron region (vv. 9–15); the southern campaign (vv. 16–17); and the coastal plain (v. 18). It is an impressive record of conquered Canaanite strongholds.

But there are two disturbing notes which indicate an emerging pattern that will grow increasingly prominent. The first is found in verse 6: Judah conquers Bezek, capturing the "king" and cutting off his thumbs and his big toes. This was an effective and brutal way of ending his military career; he could handle neither bow nor sword again. But mutilation was a pagan practice, not a biblical one. The men of Judah had been commanded to put him to death, but they were drawing their standards from the cultures around them, adopting Canaanite practices. Judah's obedience was only partial.

The second note is found in verse 19. Judah is unable to drive out the inhabitants of the plains because they have iron chariots. This seems logical—the Canaanites had superior military technology that gave them an advantage. However, Yahweh had promised that He would drive out the enemy. In fact, Joshua had declared that "though the Canaanites have chariots fitted with iron and though they are strong, you can drive them out" (Joshua 17:18). The real reason why Judah did not have victory was because they did not fully trust their God. **Diminished power is always the result of diminished faith.**

The phrase, "were unable to drive the people from the plains" (Judges 1:19), is echoed throughout the rest of the chapter. Benjamin fails to drive out the Jebusites (v. 21), while Manasseh does not drive out the pagan inhabitants (vv. 27–28). The same record is given of Ephraim (v. 29), Zebulun (v. 30), and Asher (vv. 31–32). With Dan, we reach the lowest point (vv. 34–36): they are pressed into the hill country because the Amorites won't allow them to come down to the plain.

The lesson of Judges 1 is very clear. The people of Israel deliberately chose to obey God only partially.

Rather than following the Lord wholeheartedly, they compromised. In a few short verses we have moved from conquest to compromised coexistence to capitulation. This is a pattern that will yield very bitter fruits.

How complete is your obedience to God? Are there some areas in your life where you obey Him only partially?

What are some possible ways in which Christians today might live in "compromised coexistence"?

Day 3

Read Judges 2:1–5

Gilgal was a place of great spiritual and symbolic significance. It was the Israelites' first encampment across the Jordan River (Joshua 4–5), where the Lord had commanded them to repent and to keep the terms of His covenant with Abraham by renewing the practice of circumcision and observing the Passover. It was also there that the Lord appeared to Joshua and promised that He would lead Israel into victory. Gilgal was the place of victory and blessing, of covenant renewal.

The Abrahamic covenant is extremely important because it is the key to God's programme throughout human history, and it gives Christ-followers the great assurance that God always keeps His promises.

But covenant grace involves reciprocal obligations. Worshipping God meant that the Israelites were to make no treaty alliance with the people of Canaan. Also, the sin of the Canaanites was a deadly cancer, and they were to remove it surgically from the land before it infected them (Exodus 23:32–33). Covenant faithfulness and covenant exclusivity were non-negotiables.

At the same time, God didn't issue a challenge and then leave Israel to do the best they could. When

He gives us a responsibility, He provides the resources to carry it out (Deuteronomy 28:2, 7–8). With the responsibility of unwavering obedience to the Lord comes the resource of unlimited power from Him to make it possible.

But what happened? The angel of the Lord puts it very simply: "Yet you have disobeyed me . . ." (Judges 2:2). The angel confronts the Israelites with their covenant unfaithfulness, and spells out the consequences they will encounter.

Despite their sin and unbelief, God did not turn His back on His people. He was not terminating His covenant. His coming was an act of grace, designed to bring the nation to radical repentance.

When the people realise what God is saying, they begin to weep in grief, shame, and repentance (v. 4). As a result, the place receives a new name, "Bokim", or "weeping" (v. 5). Among the greatest truths of spiritual experience is that the path of partial obedience only leads to Bokim. There is no joy in half-hearted spiritual experience.

The most miserable people in the world are professing

believers who will not commit themselves to the Lord.

Rather than experiencing the best of both worlds, they have the worst. If we try to walk the tightrope of compromise and partial obedience, we will not know spiritual victory and God's blessing, only the bitterness of defeat and frustration.

But even there the grace of God is not finished. He does not just abandon His people to suffer the consequences of sin—He calls them back to wholehearted obedience and commitment to Him.

Day 4

Church history is filled with examples of the "second-generation syndrome", and sadly so are many churches today. The parents' fervour for Christ becomes the children's formalism and the grandchildren's apathy.

Too often, the second-generation experience is a second-hand experience.

But before we examine the failure of Israel's second generation, let us reflect briefly on the impact of Joshua and his generation. They were the first generation, the standard by which we can judge the condition of the second generation.

Joshua was a great soldier, brilliant organiser, charismatic leader, and gifted administrator. But merely listing these characteristics is superficial, because none of them reveal the heart of the man. Two characteristics stand out and account for the way in which God worked through him.

The first was Joshua's responsiveness to the Word of God. As he faced the awesome task of succeeding Moses, God came to him with a promise and a challenge: "Be strong and very courageous. Be careful to obey all the law my servant Moses gave you . . . Then you will be prosperous and successful" (Joshua 1:7–8).

God promised Joshua prosperity and wisdom through obeying, reading, and proclaiming His Word. Throughout his life, Joshua acted on that promise, and God honoured his obedience.

Joshua's second outstanding characteristic was his active faith. Trusting God's promise that "I will never leave you nor forsake you" (Joshua 1:5), he guided two million people toward a river in flood, and God cut off the waters so the people could cross the Jordan on dry ground (3:14–17).

In obedience to God's orders, Joshua marched the nation around Jericho, and the walls of the city crumbled (Joshua 6:1–20). By faith, he commanded the sun to stand still over Gibeon and the moon over the valley of Aijalon, and they did (10:12–13). Believing God's promise of victory, he attacked an overwhelming military alliance at Merom and led his people in defeating their enemies (11:1–14).

Joshua was not a perfect man. But God did great deeds for His people through him, not because of Joshua's gifts and abilities, but because he trusted God and ordered his life by the Word of God. Joshua kept Israel in the place of God's blessing (v. 7).

One man, committed unreservedly to God and His Word, can make an enormous difference for good in the lives of God's people. One woman, living her life for Jesus Christ, can bring blessings to many. If you trust God and build your life on His Word, you can have a godly influence on your family, student group, or local church.

What can you do to retain "first-generation" fervour for God and His Word?

How can you apply the lessons of Joshua's faith and obedience in your life?

Day 5

How could the second generation of Israelites forget when their parents had seen and experienced so much of God's blessings?

They were not ignorant of the Exodus or the conquest. What they had not seen with their eyes, they had heard with their ears from their parents. They knew about the Lord and His deeds. But still they did not know or acknowledge Him for who He was (Judges 2:10). They became complacent and forgot how to walk in fellowship with God (v. 12). This was not merely a personal failure, but a communal one.

We need to examine the cause of this second-generation syndrome, so that we can guard against it in our lives. Three factors stand out:

One, they were satisfied with the status quo. The first generation conquered parts of Canaan, but pockets of the enemy remained. Then the second generation came along. God had given them a command to move out and take the land completely, but they refused to trust and obey. They were content and comfortable.

There is great temptation to believe that the experience of the first generation is the standard or that their ideals are beyond us, and we should settle for something less. This is wrong. The experiences of previous generations are not to be a diving board from which we can only go down, but a platform from which we climb to a higher level.

Two, they took God's blessings for granted and did not acknowledge His grace. Our attitude toward our blessings and possessions is one of the most determinative factors in our spiritual health. To be ungrateful is not only foolish but dangerous. Israel looked at the land they possessed and said, "Look at what we have accomplished!" They became self-centred, sowing the seeds of self-destruction.

That is why the Word of God commands us to give thanks in everything (1 Thessalonians 5:18). **It is essential to cultivate and nourish a spirit of praise and thanksgiving in our personal lives, families, and community of believers.** Apathy withers where praise flourishes.

Three, they neglected the statutes of God. There is almost no reference to the study of God's Word in Judges—the Israelites possessed God's Word but chose to ignore it. Ritually, they did many of the things the Law required, but their obedience was based on tradition, not on personal conviction.

There is an enormous difference between a direct and an indirect relationship to Scripture. One person peddles second-hand wisdom, things he has heard from parents, preachers, or friends. The other speaks with personal conviction, because she has been in the Word, studied and prayed about it, and heard the Shepherd's voice. Don't neglect the Word of God!

In what way can Christians today become complacent or satisfied with the status quo?

What can you thank God for today?

Day 6

Read Judges 2:11–13

At Mount Sinai, Israel entered into a covenant with God to be faithful to Him, to obey His laws, to do His will, and to reject alliances with Canaan and its gods. With the death of Joshua and the following generation, however, the last living link with Mount Sinai was gone, and the result is gross sin—not sin in general, but the sin of covenant violation (Judges 2:11–12). **The greatest sin a human being can commit is to turn one's back on the living God and serve manmade gods.**

The Canaanites believed in a number of local gods, including Baal, the god of the storm and rains, and Ashtaroth, the goddess of sensual love, fertility, and war. Followers engaged in temple prostitution, fertility rites, drunken sexual orgies, idolatry, snake-worship, homosexuality, and human sacrifice. Everything about the Canaanite religion—its view of God, moral standards, ethics and values, and rituals—stood in total contradiction to everything God had revealed about himself to His people. And yet its appeal to some of our most human drives and urges is obvious.

The Israelites did the unthinkable. They did not forget Yahweh entirely, but borrowed the rites, practices, and idols of Canaanite paganism and grafted them onto their existing worship to create a new, syncretistic religion. Why? How could a people who had witnessed the power of God drift so far from Him? It did not happen all at once.

Assimilation is not an overnight process, but a gradual one. First there is the acceptance of alien ideas, values, and practices. This is followed by the abandonment of certain native ideas, values, and practices in order to accommodate the new ones. Third, there is growing adaptation to the surrounding culture, until finally there is virtual capitulation to what was once completely foreign and alien. How did this happen?

One, they lost fellowship with God by incomplete obedience. When Israel did not drive out the people as God commanded, they sowed the seeds of their own spiritual failure.

Two, they did not consciously remind themselves of the grace of God. They forsook God when they forgot all that He had done for them.

Three, they rejected the Word of God. Israel began to look at life the way the Canaanites did. Instead of being controlled by the truths of Scripture, they were controlled by the desires and impulses of their sinful natures.

We too will suffer what the Israelites experienced
if we follow in their footsteps. Galatians 6:8
reminds us that when we sow to please the flesh
we reap from the flesh; and its harvest is corruption
and decay.

Day 7

Read Judges 2:14–15

As Christians, we must never forget that God and evil cannot co-exist. Because of the Lord Jesus, we know that God's anger blazed out at Calvary, and we believers are spared from His wrath. But it is impossible for us to live in sin and have fellowship with God. The disciplining hand of God will work in our lives if we choose sin in deliberate disobedience to Him. Sin that is not confessed to the Lord brings servitude and bondage.

God had promised victory to Israel if she trusted in Him. But when she turned away from God, she inevitably condemned herself to defeat and bondage. Over 300 years, she was repeatedly plundered, and her people enslaved and oppressed (Judges 2:14). In addition to external oppression, they were afflicted with inner decay. Sin produces servitude.

But God's grace is triumphant over people's sin. Although He allows His people to experience servitude, He does not abandon them to it. Following sin and servitude, comes supplication. Chapter 2 has no direct reference to Israel calling out to God; verse 18 only tells us that "the LORD had compassion on them as they groaned under those who oppressed and afflicted them". However, five times within Judges (3:9; 3:15; 4:3; 6:6; 10:10) the people cry out to the Lord in their servitude, and each time that supplication marks the beginning of their deliverance.

We often live in our weakness, ignoring God's presence until all the threads begin to unravel. Then, in our desperation, we call out, praying and begging for Him to intervene and put the pieces back together again. This kind of prayer can be a life-changing experience that turns everything around. Or it can be a shallow, superficial call for help, forgotten as soon as things improve.

In fact, the latter is what we see consistently throughout Judges. Not once is the people's prayer one of genuine repentance. They groan over the consequences of their sin, but not over the fact of their sin. They regret the consequences, but do not repent of the cause.

The amazing fact is that, no matter how deep our sin or how shallow our prayer, God hears us. Each time His people call, God hears and intervenes. Not once does He refuse or turn His back. He does not condition His help on their improvement or on their past record, but on their need. The throne we approach in prayer is a throne of grace, where we receive mercy and find grace to help in time of need (Hebrews 4:16).

ThinkThrough

How did you
respond the last time
God answered your
prayer for help? How
did the experience
change you?

What can you do to
remain in an attitude
of thankfulness for
God's mercy and
grace?

Day 8

Read Judges 2:16–18

Whenever the Israelites turn to God in their servitude, He brings about their deliverance by raising up a total of twelve men and one woman, traditionally called judges.

This word conveys to us the image of a courtroom judge. But these "judges" had no courtroom, wore no robes, and set no laws. Although they may have had some civil functions, they were military rather than judicial figures. Their primary function was to deliver the Israelites from the hands of those who had plundered them (v.16, NKJV)—they led the people against the enemy; then provided civil justice and leadership, settled disputes, and trusted in God to deal with problems. God also intended for them to be spiritual leaders within the nation, although nearly all of them were conspicuous failures in this regard.

Verse 18 gives three significant facts about the judges. First, God raised them up. They were not appointed by other human authorities or elected; they were divinely appointed. Second, God was with them. The ministry of the Holy Spirit was at work in their lives as God empowered them to carry out their tasks. This did not result in changed character—it was only power and enablement for a specific task. Third, God worked through the judges.

They were channels for His activity. They were His gift to His people.

Some of them are designated "major judges" because they served as political liberators and military leaders—Othniel, Ehud, Deborah and Barak, Gideon, Jephthah, and Samson. Other judges served as local leaders or preservers of the peace, and are designated "minor judges" —Shamgar, Tola, Jair, Ibzan, Elon, and Abdon.

During this period, Israel was a theocracy. There was a minimal form of government, and the major leaders were directly raised up and empowered by God, and answerable to Him. He was king in Israel.

Why did God raise up the judges? It would have been much easier to discard a people with a record of consistent failure. But God does not break His covenants, and He does not desert His people. In fact, as the people experience their rightly deserved judgment, we read, "the LORD relented because of their groaning" (v. 18).

What a beautiful insight into the heart of God! His people sin against Him. They rebel against Him and spurn His love. If God said, "That's enough", justice would have had no complaint.

But when God saw Israel wallowing in her bondage of sin, His heart was moved with pity and love. Judges is full of the grace of God, the same grace and love that ultimately sent Jesus to the cross. **His love keeps reaching out and out, even to the uttermost cost of Calvary.**

ThinkThrough

Think about the times God had reached out to you despite your failures and disobedience.

How would you respond to His love and mercy today?

Day 9

God's love is accepted and used, then discarded like a worn-out shoe. The judge passes away, but the people have not learned their lesson. Once again the whole dreary pattern repeats itself (Judges 2:19, 3:5–6). That is the incessant pattern of the book of Judges—sin, servitude, supplication, salvation, and downward spiral.

In perfect justice, the Lord declares his verdict (2:21). He will not deliver Israel from the Canaanites, but will use them to test His people (2:22; 3:1, 4) and remind Israel that she remains God-dependent. He will also use them to teach her war, to toughen her up for His ultimate purposes. It is an eloquent reminder that sin is always a serious matter for the children of God. If we do not deal decisively with sin in our lives, we will never experience the fullness of God's blessing. There can be no compromise, no peaceful co-existence with sin. If we try to go part-way in our commitment to God, we will quickly find ourselves caught in a downward spiral.

But God does not leave the second generation to wallow in their apathy. His strategy for moving them forward is spelled out in Judges 3:1–2. He allows pockets of resistance to remain. Why? God desires a group of people who know how to trust Him in battle, people who will aggressively pursue His agenda. Victory does not come from human courage or wisdom or skill; it comes from a faithful God.

Have you ever wondered why God does not take away your sinful nature? Why there are so many areas of weakness in your life, and such difficult problems and obstacles for you to overcome? Why are there so many needs around for you to fill? Are you ever perplexed by the persistence of unsolved problems in even the most biblically-faithful fellowships?

Part of the answer is found in Judges 3:2. The Lord uses those difficulties to teach us how to wage spiritual war. He wants to shake us out of our apathy and teach us to trust Him. **Often it is only when the enemy has completely overrun us, and all our resources are gone, that we develop a teachable spirit.** These times of failure and crisis become teaching times as the Lord shows us how to make war—how to trust in Him.

The implication of this strategy for our lives is clear: we cannot stand still in our Christian experience. If we try to stand still, we can be sure that the principalities and powers arrayed against us will not. Either we advance, or we perish.

ThinkThrough

Read Romans 8:28. How might God be teaching us through adversities in our lives?

What lessons can you learn from the "pockets of resistance" in your life?

Day 10

Read Judges 3:7–31

Many Christians are paralysed by a belief that they do not fit the mould of a person God would use. They have an image of the kind of person the Lord would choose to be His servant, and see themselves as being a long way off. But when we turn to God's Word, we discover a delightful truth. God uses people of all kinds, shapes, and colours, and has a unique purpose for each one of us. Consider the first three judges:

Othniel (Judges 3:7–11) came from a family led by an outstanding believer (v. 9). He was a skilful, courageous, and proven leader, and a man of personal faith. But the key to his accomplishments is found in verse 10: "the Spirit of the LORD came upon him". Othniel did not derive his strength from his family background or his character, but from the Holy Spirit's enablement.

Ehud (vv. 12–30) was a man with a limitation—he was "a left-handed man" (v. 15). This was considered a weakness in battle: a left-hander in the ranks would disrupt the entire formation. Ehud could have been devastated by this problem. Instead, he not only accepted it, but turned it into a tool to be used for God. He concealed his sword on the right side of his body—something no one would expect—and was able to elude normal security precautions (v. 16) and kill the king of Moab.

Shamgar (v. 31) was a peasant, as his weapon suggests—an ox goad is used by peasants working with oxen in the fields. He was also a man of courage: only a very brave person takes on 600 men armed with nothing but an ox goad. We are given no further details about how he performed such an amazing feat; all we know is that Shamgar's courage must have been born of his faith in God.

God uses different kinds of people: He uses Othniels, Ehuds, Shamgars, and He will use you too if you would only trust in Him. God uses people who draw their strength from Him: those who wait for the Lord will exchange their weakness for His strength (Isaiah 40:29–31). And God uses people who step out in faith and trust Him: the three judges had the courage to take a risk for God, and were bold enough to trust in God's promises of victory and confront the enemy.

Whoever you are, God has a place for you. Your limitations are not a problem for Him. Accept yourself—not your sins, but your limitations. God does. **Step out in faith to see Him accept you as a**

unique individual and work through you for His glory.

Day 11

Read Judges 4:1–9

Once again the people of Israel are forced to learn the principle Jesus taught in John 8:34: "Everyone who sins is a slave to sin." For 20 years, the northern tribes have been oppressed severely by Jabin and Sisera (Judges 4:2–3). But Israel's real problem is spiritual, not military. Its real need is a living faith in God. If the Israelites would trust Him, He would deliver them from the most impossible situation. To teach the Israelites that, God does a very unusual thing: He chooses a woman to deliver His people.

Deborah is one of the only three prophetesses in the Old Testament, and the only woman ever called by God to be the national leader of His people. She is a leader of distinction from whom we can learn a great deal:

First, she sees a need and is committed to doing something about it. She is not the only one to see the desperate need in the lives of her people, but she is the only one who is determined to do something about it (Judges 5:6–7).

Second, she enlists help (4:6). Deborah is realistic: Israel has a military problem, and she needs a military leader to do what she cannot. Therefore she sends north for Barak, a distinguished soldier. She is wise enough to know the value of a team and perceptive enough to recognise both her own limitations and Barak's strengths.

Third, she motivates him (vv. 6–9). Barak is apparently wrapped up in fear and uncertainty, and Deborah sets out to encourage and motivate him. She challenges him with God's command, strengthens him with God's promise, and encourages him with her presence.

Fourth, she develops a plan (vv. 6–7). Almost anyone can see a need, but it is another thing to come up with a plan to deal with it. She tells Barak to recruit 10,000 men from Naphtali and Zebulun and have them march to Mount Tabor.

Deborah demonstrated outstanding talents as a leader. But it was only by faith in God that she carried out her plans and reached her goal. Her faith shone through her challenge to Barak (vv. 6–7) and motivated him (v. 14).

The most important characteristic of a Christian leader is a dynamic, bold faith in God. We may have all the leadership principles, but if we do not trust God or live in personal fellowship with Jesus, we will be a failure as an elder, teacher, parent, or disciple-maker. What the people we lead need more than anything else is a person who knows his God.

As a parent, church leader, or disciple-maker, what practical lessons of leadership can you learn from Deborah?

How can you remind yourself to keep trusting in God?

Day 12

God uses Deborah to prepare Barak. Then she steps into the background, and Barak moves up into the foreground (Judges 4:15–16). He goes to the tribes of Zebulun and Naphtali, who have been most affected by the occupation, and recruits 10,000 men (v. 10). Then they march out to Mount Tabor, where Sisera meets him with 900 iron chariots and a huge army.

Now let us review the situation. Israel is outmanned: Sisera has considerably more than 10,000 men, since usually only a very small, elite percentage of an army would be riding in chariots. Israel is out-supplied: Sisera has 900 iron chariots (v. 13), while Israel does not even have spears and shields. And Israel is out-positioned: sending ill-equipped foot soldiers against chariots on a flat plain would amount to mass suicide.

Yet that is exactly what God commands His people to do (v. 14). It is not really Barak's strategy or Deborah's plan at all; it is God's. He wants to teach His people that it is not chariots or troop numbers that makes the difference; it is He.

What happens? We read that "the LORD routed Sisera" (v. 15). The word means "to cause confusion"—the same word used to describe God's intervention against the Egyptians in Exodus 14:24. How does He do that? Judges 5:21 gives us a clue. At this time of the year, the Kishon would normally be a dried-up creek bed. But God causes a violent storm to sweep through the area, turning the ground into a muddy quagmire, bogging down the chariots. Chaos ensues, Sisera's army panics and breaks ranks, and the Israelites defeat them.

Then God intervenes in another way. Fleeing the defeat, Sisera stumbles into the tent of a non-Israelite woman named Jael, where he expects to find safety (v. 17). But Jael acts in a way that was a shocking violation of Middle Eastern standards of hospitality and treaty obligation (v. 21). The irony is that it was not a valiant warrior like Barak who conquered the great general Sisera, but a pagan woman, using a woman's tools.

Surely God was saying something to His people, both then and now, by that strange twist of events. "If you will trust in me, I will deal with the Siseras in your life. And I do not need a man of great strength to do it; I can use a Jael. You only need me!"

Our eyes need to be focused on God. When Israel trusted God, their enemy was defeated. That is why the writer summarises the entire account by saying "On that day God subdued Jabin king of Canaan before the Israelites" (v. 23). **The essence of godly leadership is an unswerving commitment to being God's servant.**

What kind of "Siseras" do you face in life? How are you responding?

As a leader, is God telling you to do something that doesn't make sense by worldly logic?

Day 13

Read Judges 5:1–13

The Song of Deborah celebrates the day God gave Israel victory over Jabin and Sisera. This hymn of praise is not only a great and complex piece of Hebrew poetry, but it also gives a theological interpretation of the victory, providing profound insight into the spiritual warfare that believers are engaged in today. It also establishes an important principle: God's blessing needs to be received and celebrated with gratitude. **When God does something for us, the natural response of our hearts should be to praise Him and acknowledge publicly what He has done.**

Verses 1–5 form the introduction to Deborah's song by celebrating the God of Israel, who had powerfully displayed His greatness. He is the hero of the story, the giver of victory, the object of trust, the proper recipient of praise. Because Israel's view of God was distorted, they had been easy prey for the temptations of pagan gods. Therefore Deborah focuses their attention where it ought to be—on the character of Israel's great God.

In verses 6–12, she looks back to the times of desperation (vv. 6–7), into which God had intervened with decisive power. How had Israel ended up in such trouble? Because they

"chose new gods" (v. 8, NLT); the people had turned away from God, and as a result the power of God had gone from them.

Then, although He had every reason to abandon them, God reached out in love to Israel and raised up Deborah. Under the Lord's guidance, she recruited Barak and gave him God's plan for the military campaign (Judges 4:6–7). The heart of that plan—to recruit 10,000 men and attack Sisera—sounds simple, but it was not. Sisera was enormously powerful, while the Israelites were virtually unarmed. How could one recruit 10,000 men, just to march them towards almost certain death?

The astonishing thing is that fear of the terrible odds wasn't a problem— the people responded eagerly and enthusiastically (vv. 2, 9, 13). Three features stand out:

One, there was a spontaneous response (v. 2). The people came freely, voluntarily, and eagerly. There was no conscription, coercion, or bribery to compel warriors to enlist. There was a challenge from the heart of God and a free, spontaneous, and unhesitating response to that challenge.

Two, there was a practical response (v. 9). The people were not just moved emotionally, they also acted. They may not have been a powerful and seasoned fighting force, but they were willing warriors, ready to do battle under the banner of their God.

Three, there was an individual response (v. 13). Neither the leaders nor the peasants stood back to let the others fight. Everyone faced up to his responsibility before God.

ThinkThrough

How can we remind ourselves to praise God and acknowledge publicly what He has done?

Is your response to God's call to action like that of Israel? How can you cultivate such a heart that responds freely, voluntarily, and eagerly?

Day 14

Deborah is not content simply to record the general principles of the response. In precise detail, she lists the tribes that came and characterised their response. Three tribes deserve special attention. The men of Issachar (Judges 5:15) rushed into battle at Barak's heels. Zebulun "risked their very lives" (v. 18). And Naphtali (v. 18) chose the most difficult part of the battle. We must measure ourselves against this kind of commitment—wholehearted, spontaneous, enthusiastic, and daring —which obeys God's command and marches into the teeth of the enemy.

Do we see that kind of response to Jesus' call to be His disciples today— engaging in spiritual warfare, living for Him in the world, and serving Him in different ways? Or do we give only the spare parts of our lives to Jesus? If we are not careful, we may end up with much duty and little love in our service to the King.

Not all the tribes responded. Four-and-a-half tribes chose not to come, and represent different forms of the reluctant spirit that paralyses our Christian service.

The men of Reuben (vv. 15–16) were emotionally stirred, but their feet never proceeded. It is easy to have great "searching of heart", but harder to translate emotion into action and head off to battle.

Gilead (v. 17), which included Gad and half of Manasseh, had cut themselves off from active fellowship with the other tribes. Today, that would be like living outside of active church fellowship despite the Lord's exhortation to continue meeting (Hebrews 10:25). Love for fellow believers is an evidence of salvation (see 1 John 3:10, 14).

Dan lacked spiritual growth. They had never realised their potential under God. All they could see was their own situation, so they stayed where they were. A Christian who does not have a growing Christian life will not have a volunteering, eager spiritual experience.

The people of Asher were focused entirely on their work—their ships, docks, and trading. They had no vision for God's work, no sense of the significance they had in God's programme, and no understanding of the mission God had called them to.

None of these four-and-a-half tribes ever again made a significant contribution to the cause of God. Asher virtually vanished, Dan nosedived into apostasy (giving up on God), and the two-and-a-half tribes were repeatedly overrun. They lived for themselves, refusing to risk what they had, and, as a result, lost what they had. **If we do not have an eager, giving heart for God, our reluctant spirit will affect fellow believers. But above all, it will injure us as we shrivel up inside our shell.**

How would you characterise your response to God's call? Is it reluctant or enthusiastic?

How can you apply the lessons from the responses of Issachar, Zebulun, and Naphtali?

Day 15

The precise identity and location of the town of Meroz are unclear, but it was an Israelite town that chose to sit out the battle. It wasn't simply that they didn't come to the aid of Deborah and Barak—Meroz is cursed because they did not come "to help the Lord" (Judges 5:23).

The Lord does not need our help. But He desires it.

Going to war was aligning oneself with the cause of the King. The volunteering tribes knew they were helping the Lord, and, in doing so, they were serving the Lord. When you feel frustration, discouragement, bitterness, or complacency settling in, stop and remind yourself that you are not doing it for people—you are doing it for your Saviour. Do you view your service like that—as an act of love done for the Lord? When you adopt that perspective on service, it has a revolutionary impact on your life.

We should seek to emulate the motivation of the volunteers (v. 31). They were the righteous part of the nation who, in a day of apostasy, knew what it was to love God.

When our hearts belong to God, we begin to serve Him enthusiastically, spontaneously, and freely. It is not the quantity of our service that is really decisive, but the quality of our relationship with the Lord. Love for Jesus Christ produces service befitting the King.

A giving, volunteering spirit also produces a joyful heart. Deborah and these volunteers are singing because they know the joy of giving to the Lord. Joy in a believer's life is never simply a product of receiving. It is the result of giving themselves to the Lord and knowing the overflow of His love in their lives.

The children of Israel had a most unusual rule of war: "Is anyone afraid or faint-hearted? Let him go home so that his fellow soldiers will not become disheartened too" (Deuteronomy 20:8). How do you think that rule would work in our society? But God was trying to teach His people an important lesson. "I want volunteers in my army, people who will serve me freely, eagerly, and spontaneously."

That is what He says to us today. In fact, we can capture the theme of Deborah's song by adopting the familiar words of 2 Corinthians 9:7: "Each of you should give what you have decided in your heart to give, not reluctantly or under compulsion, for God loves a cheerful giver." Does that describe your spirit in your service? Jesus is looking for people with the committed hearts of Issachar, Zebulun, and Naphtali. Are you rushing into battle at your Saviour's heels?

How will seeing our service as an act of love to the Lord change our attitude towards it?

How can you encourage someone who is frustrated or discouraged in his service at church?

Day 16

Read Judges 6:1–10

Once again, we see the distressing cycle of sin, servitude, supplication, and salvation. Once again, the people take their eyes off the Lord and focus on the idols and evils of Baal worship, and once again, God gives them over to the consequence of their sin—bondage and servitude under a foreign nation (Judges 6:1).

This time God uses an alliance of desert peoples led by the Midianites, a Bedouin people from the Arabian Desert. The Midianites had a unique strategy. Rather than invading and occupying the land, they simply waited until the Israelites had done all the hard work of planting the crops. Then they would move in and swoop through the land, stripping it bare of grain, vegetables, fruit, and livestock. Finally, loaded with spoil, they would return to the desert and wait until the next harvest time (vv. 3–5).

This pattern of seasonal invasion is repeated for seven years, crushing Israelite morale and ravaging their economy (vv. 1–2). Finally, the burden becomes too great and they cry out to the LORD (v. 6). Once again, however, it is a cry that lacked repentance. The Israelites call on God, but they have not dealt with their sin. Baal worship still abounds in the land (v. 10).

Until now, every time God's people had called to Him, He had sent a judge—a deliverer—to change their condition. Not this time. God sends a prophet because His people need repentance more than they need relief. His message is one of condemnation, not comfort; of judgment, not encouragement.

The prophet begins by reminding them of God's unchanging faithfulness and grace (vv. 8–9). God had delivered them from Egypt, given them Canaan, and entered into a covenant with them (vv. 9–10). Yet, deliberately and defiantly, Israel broke it. God states the obvious: "You have not listened to me" (v. 10). (It could be translated as, "You have not obeyed me.") Strangely, there is no pronouncement of judgment or consequences, only a reminder that the Israelites had brought it on themselves. **They are what they are and where they are because they had turned away from the living God.**

All too often, when Christians experience the consequences of their own sinful or foolish choices, they complain, "How could God let this happen to me? This isn't fair!" We need to remember that the one thing none of us really wants from God is justice. If we were to get what we truly deserve, each one of us would be in terrible trouble!

Day 17

There was never a less likely liberator. Gideon means "hacker" in Hebrew, so he was apparently a man of physical strength. But the man we meet certainly does not present us with a picture of strength. Normally, a person would thresh wheat on a floor in an exposed place so that the wind would carry away the lighter chaff. Gideon is furtively beating out a few sheaves of wheat in a sheltered winepress under a tree because he is afraid that the Midianites would confiscate his meagre supply (Judges 6:11). He is a defeated, discouraged man, filled with doubts and fears. He is no "mighty warrior" (v. 12)—but that is exactly what he is going to become, because the Lord is with him.

God often deals with people in this way. By His power, a childless, 99-year-old Abraham had a son (Genesis 21:2), and an impetuous, emotionally unstable Peter was transformed into a pillar of the early church (Galatians 2:9). Other people see our flaws and failings, but God sees our possibilities through His transforming presence. When God looks at us, He does not see us for what we are, but for what we can become through His work in our lives. He takes weak, insignificant people and transforms them by His presence. He knows our weaknesses, failures, discouragements, doubts, and inadequacies, and comes to us with the promise of His power that will transform our inadequacy into His strength.

When Gideon expresses his concerns (v. 13), the Lord responds: "Go in the strength you have" (v. 14). This God-given strength accompanies both God's command and His promise (vv. 12, 14, 16). God is calling Gideon to go forward on the basis of the strength that He always supplies for His commission. If we look to our own strength, we will always end up in defeat, or perhaps worse, in self-deceiving arrogance. God's answer is not positive thinking, but the promise of His presence, provision, and power. When the Lord commissions us, He promises to be with us always (Matthew 28:18–20).

Gideon is also filled with a deep sense of personal inadequacy and insignificance. "How can I do that?" he asks. "The job's too big for me. I have no qualifications, and I do not have any support" (v. 15, paraphrased). This is exactly where God begins with a person. Time and time again, we see the Lord cutting away a person's self-confidence to bring him to the place where he admits that he is totally inadequate to do or to be what God desires. Then

He confronts the person with the truth of His total adequacy: "I will be with you" (v. 6).

Inadequate in ourselves, we are overwhelmingly adequate through our God.

Day 18

By now Gideon has come to realise that there is something special about the "angel of the Lord". To be sure, he decides to honour his guest and seek a sign that He is really God's messenger (Judges 6:17–18). This is a time of famine, yet Gideon prepares a feast (v. 19). It must have been extremely costly and taken a considerable time to prepare. When Gideon brings the offering to the "angel", the Lord takes control. Fire, a common sign of God's presence, devours the food (v. 21). Not even a doubter like Gideon could miss that message. He instantly knows that he is in the presence of God. Feeling instinctively the depths of his own sin and guilt as well as his mortality, he cries out in fear (v. 22).

God has not come to judge Gideon but to deliver His people, so He speaks with words He often uses when people are alarmed to realise they are in His presence (v. 23). In response, Gideon builds an altar, a sign of God's encounter with him. This is a major step forward for Gideon's fledgling faith. He is going public and declaring his identity as a follower of Yahweh. And this is in Ophrah, the site of a major Baal shrine sponsored by Gideon's own father (v. 25).

The mark of fire on the rock and the stones are reminders of God's promises. And on the basis of those promises, Gideon will receive power to take on his mission. In the same way, etched in the Word of God are the promises of God's presence. They are written in the indelible ink of God's faithfulness, and when we apply those promises to our lives, we are transformed.

On his own, Gideon was a weak, faltering, doubting man. But he had first-hand contact with the Lord, and he was never quite the same again. He had a long way to go, but the journey had begun. He was a new man, transformed by God's presence. God had taught Gideon that it was not his inadequacy but God's adequacy that really counted.

God is in the process of transforming people, and He does it when we spend time with Him (see 2 Corinthians 3:18). There is no need to look for His message in visions; the faith has been delivered to us and recorded in God's Word (Jude 3). Scripture contains everything we need to be complete and equipped for every good work (2 Timothy 3:16–17). Through His Word, we behold the glory of the Lord Jesus, and as we see Him face to face, we are changed. But we must spend time with Him. Only that will truly equip us to serve Him.

Are you spending time "looking at the Lord" through His Word?

How can you allow God to transform you?

Day 19

Read Judges 6:25–26

Gideon's own backyard contains a visible symbol of all that is wrong in the nation of Israel. God had made it very clear that there were to be no rival altars, idols, or other gods. But Gideon's father Joash has a pagan shrine on his property (Judges 6:25).

God's will is clear: until Gideon puts things right in his own backyard, God will not and cannot use him to deliver His people. He cannot fight for the Lord while retaining a shrine to Baal. The Lord's instructions are straightforward. Gideon is to tear down the altar, chop down the Asherah, and sacrifice a bull on a brand new altar for the Lord (vv. 25–26). The two altars cannot co-exist.

There are also some profound spiritual implications for Gideon's assignment:

First, Baal must go before Midian can go. Before Gideon can be the deliverer of Israel, he has to be the destroyer of the false god Baal. It is the same for us. Before we can have victory over our sins, problems, or habits, Jesus Christ must be the unquestioned Lord of our lives. There is no victory where there is idolatry or a divided heart. There can be no compromise if we desire to know the Lord at work in our lives. What might be the Baal or the Asherah in your life? Many things can be good and valuable in themselves, until they take the place that belongs only to the Lord. They must be chopped down before God will deal with the Midian in your life.

Second, God's altar cannot be built until Baal's altar is destroyed. The two cannot co-exist. The Lord will not allow any mixing or syncretism. There can be no worship acceptable to God until we remove the false altars from our hearts and lives. God alone must be Lord and King. In our pluralistic, inclusive age, syncretism is a constant temptation. Our postmodern society has a "both-and" mind-set that resents and even rejects "either-or" thinking. It loves to keep its options open. It embraces uncertainty and personal choice and hates the idea of absolute truths. It wants to try to hold together opposites and have it both ways. But the Lord will not tolerate such an arrangement, either in Gideon's day or in ours.

Third, the place we must start is in our own backyard. Before Gideon can lead his whole nation to faith in God, he has to deal with the Baal in his family. That is a principle that runs through all Scripture. If our commitment to the lordship of Jesus Christ does not first affect our home life, it will lack credibility. Begin at home first!

What "false altars" might be taking the place of God in your life?

How can we keep our faith pure in a pluralistic world that embraces the mixing of faiths?

Day 20

Read Judges 6:27–32

In many ways, God is asking Gideon to fight his most difficult battle first. Often the hardest place to represent Christ is in our own family and with our closest friends and co-workers. It is much easier to stand up for the Lord among strangers than in our own homes, communities, or companies. It is much easier to share the gospel anonymously or with casual acquaintances than with fellow workers, classmates, or close friends. But we cannot hide our commitment to the Lord from those closest to us.

Judges 6:27 conveys an important lesson about faith and obedience. God does not supernaturally remove Gideon's anxieties and fears, but Gideon obeys anyway. **Faith is not obeying without fear; it is obeying despite fear.** Trust is not demonstrated by fearlessness but by obedience. Often, God's call in our lives can stretch us to the breaking point, and we find ourselves full of fear and uncertainty. Still, God calls us to obey, and we discover that when we focus on obedience, He deals with our fears. If you sometimes feel fearful and weak as you obey God, you are in good company. Gideon's obedience, even in the darkness of night, produces results visible in the daylight of the next morning:

First is the anger of the townspeople (vv. 28–30). Verse 30 is probably the most graphic picture of the total apostasy of Israel in the book of Judges. Israel has profaned and degraded God's name; the makers of idols should have been executed. Yet the townsfolk are ready to kill Gideon. Destroying a Baal shrine is, in their opinion, a capital offence. How twisted their perspective has become!

Second is the transformation of Joash (v. 31). When Joash realises what Gideon has done, he immediately springs to his son's defence. Perhaps he was shamed and challenged morally and spiritually: he knows Gideon's actions are right and that he should have done the same thing. The man that Gideon fears the most has become his greatest advocate. Our obedience to the Lord can do great things in the lives of the most unexpected people. People whose reactions we fear the most are often the first to respond positively when they see the reality of our commitment to Jesus Christ.

Third is the reputation of Gideon (v. 32). Gideon's new name, Jerubbaal, literally means "Let Baal contend (against Gideon)", but it came to have the extended meaning "Baal-fighter" or "Baal-conqueror". Every time men looked at Gideon, they had visible proof of the weakness of Baal and the power of God. Our courage to commit ourselves decisively and finally to the lordship of Jesus Christ can be used by God in the lives of others.

ThinkThrough

How can you share your commitment to the Lord at home, in your community or workplace?

How can you draw on God's strength to obey Him despite your fears?

Day 21

Read Judges 6:33–35

Gideon has come a long way from the weak, defeated man we first met in Judges 6:11. Empowered by God's Holy Spirit and roused to action, he sounds the war trumpet, and the entire region rallies to him (vv. 33–35). The same Abiezrites who were prepared to kill Gideon for his destruction of the Baal shrine are now willing to follow, and his influence has grown (vv. 34–35).

The source of this influence is clear. The writer uses picturesque language—"the Spirit of the LORD clothed Gideon" (v. 34 ESV)—to describe a man putting on his clothes (Genesis 28:20) or a warrior putting on a suit of armour (Isaiah 59:17). What a delightful picture! The Holy Spirit takes possession, indwelling and empowering him. We saw similar language in Othniel's life (Judges 3:10), and will see it again in Jephthah (11:29) and Samson (13:25; 14:6; 15:14).

We can learn two lessons from the way God worked in Gideon's life. First, the Holy Spirit does not destroy our individuality. When Gideon was indwelt by the Spirit, he remained Gideon. He did not become Othniel, Samson, or Jephthah. **The Holy Spirit does not bring a dull conformity into our lives, but rather the power to be what God calls us uniquely to be.**

Second, the ministry of the Holy Spirit is directly related to obedience. We are commanded in Ephesians 5:18 to "be filled with the Spirit" so that certain results might follow. In Colossians 3:16, we are told to "let the message of Christ dwell among you richly," and the same results follow. There is an intimate connection between the filling of the Spirit and obeying God's Word; the picture of the Holy Spirit clothing Gideon immediately following Gideon's act of obedience suggests that same connection.

There were three things that produced changes in Gideon's life: He had first-hand contact with the Lord (Judges 6:11); he decisively and publicly committed himself to the Lord by an act of obedience (v. 27); and he came under the control of the Holy Spirit (v. 34). It was not by might or power, but by God's Spirit that Gideon was equipped to serve God.

The Spirit's ministry is essential in our lives if we are to accomplish anything of value. Just as Gideon's rallying of the Israelites and his victory was directly due to the Spirit of God, our effectiveness is directly dependent upon Him. The same Holy Spirit who clothed Gideon has come to indwell us as children of God. We are His temple, His dwelling place (1 Corinthians 6:19).

Day 22

Read Judges 6:36–40

Many Christians try to discover the will of God through fleece-setting. They say something like, "Father, if you want me to follow Plan A, please do the following by Tuesday. If you don't, I will follow Plan B." Despite the obvious fallacy of thinking that the Lord only has two options in mind, there is something to be said for a Christian who is deeply concerned about doing what the Lord wants.

But fleece-setting is not God's way of directing His children. And it is fundamentally wrong. We need to look carefully at this passage to discover why that is so:

One, Gideon was not ignorant of God's will. He knew very well what God had said He would do and what He wanted Gideon to do ("you will save Israel by my hand", Judges 6:36). Gideon wasn't really seeking to know God's will; his problem was not one of knowledge, but of faith and obedience.

Two, fleece setting is evidence of doubt, not faith. The "if" in verse 37 is thunderous. Gideon is, in effect, saying, "I know your command and your promise. But I'm sorry. That's not enough. I'm not sure I'm prepared to really believe you." When we start fleece-setting, we are really doubting the promises of God, refusing to rest in His Word, and demanding that the Lord lead us on our terms, not His. Three, fleece-setting is dictating to God. Gideon had not come to the Lord and opened his heart with his fears and doubts. Instead, he came and said, "God, here is my program. You do this and this, and I want it looked after by tomorrow morning." Gideon wanted the sovereign God to do what he said by his schedule, or he wouldn't cooperate.

Four, fleece-setting does not really solve the problem. The next morning, Gideon sees that the fleece is wet and the ground is dry (v. 38). But then he thinks: "How do I really know this was of God? Maybe it was just a coincidence." Doubt plagues him, so he goes to God again with the second test (v. 39). **The problem with fleece-setting is that it doesn't produce the certainty it promises, and it puts God into our little mental box.**

There is one beautiful lesson, however, from this story, and it is found in verse 40: "That night God did so." Those words are full of the grace of God. Gideon was a special student in God's slow-learner class. He was still saying "if" and putting out tests, but God kept on loving and working with him. What a wonderful God we slow learners have!

ThinkThrough

What does the Bible say about the revealed will of God? See Psalms 40:8; Matthew 28:18–20; Romans 12:1–2; 1 Thessalonians 5:16–18.

How will you respond to God's will?

Day 23

Read Judges 7:1–8

Few military upsets are more astonishing than the one God accomplishes through Gideon. Outnumbered 450 to 1, Gideon's army crushes the powerful hosts of Midian (Judges 7:22). But first, God has to teach Gideon and his army the value of radical dependence on Him.

The Midianites had deployed a force of 135,000 in the Valley of Jezreel, while across the plain, Gideon's men huddled behind the appropriately-named "spring of trembling (Harod)", their major water supply (v. 1). To drink, a man had to go down in full view of the enemy, and he would be reminded of how imposing the mission was. Gideon's men, numbering 32,000, had no successful experience of warfare and virtually no weapons. Imagine his feelings: "We don't have a chance. There simply aren't enough of us!" But the Lord says, "Gideon, you have too many people. We need to cut down on your numbers" (v. 2, paraphrased).

This is a fundamental spiritual principle. God is not interested simply in giving us victory and prosperity; He is concerned with teaching us trust. In fact, if our victories make us self-reliant, they will become more dangerous. That is why He demands a troop reduction—that Israel may not boast against God that her own strength has saved her (v. 2, see 2 Chronicles 26:15–16).

We cannot be too small for God to use, but we can be too big. If we want to take credit for what God is doing, God will not use us. This is why we see God working in a powerful way in the lives of weak and inadequate people. Our greatest need is not to believe that we can do it, but that our God can. Do you feel insignificant? Are you discouraged because you have no prominent gifts? Praise God! You are just the kind of person God delights to use.

God's tests to reduce Gideon's army (vv. 3, 5) also reveal what He looks for in the people He uses.

The first tests fearlessness (v. 3). God promises His presence and power, but if our fear persists, He will not force us to fight. In fact, He removes us, because fear is contagious. It focuses on the problem, not on God.

The second tests vigilance (v. 5). The men's manner of drinking reveals their attitude to the enemy. The majority fall flat on their faces and drink; for the moment, they forget all about Midian. But 300 men kneel, probably holding their spears in one hand while scooping water with the other. They will not take their eyes off the enemy; they will not forget their central purpose.

God is not looking for great Christians, but for fervent, wholehearted believers who want their lives to count for Him.

How can you remind yourself to depend on God, and not on your own strength?

Think about your commitment to Jesus Christ. Is it characterised by fearlessness?

Day 24

Read Judges 7:8–22

When God comes again to Gideon with a command and a promise, He knows that Gideon needs to have his courage shored up (Judges 7:9). So He sends Gideon and Purah into the Midianite camp, where they hear two men talking about a dream (v. 13).

This is a beautiful example of God's sovereignty. He directs Gideon and Purah so they come to precisely the right tent at exactly the right time, and plants both the dream and its interpretation in the Midianites' heads. And it is then that Gideon learns the greatest lesson of his life: this is not a battle between 300 Israelites and 135,000 Midianites; it is God fighting Midian. For the first time, Gideon comes to realise the greatness of God, and he worships (v. 15). We are never truly prepared for battle until we know what it is to bow in worship before God (see Daniel 11:32).

God has also set up the Midianites by planting fear in their hearts (vv. 14, 22). Their concern is irrational—why should an army of 135,000 fear an army of 300? The only answer is that God has already prepared Midian for Gideon. **When God calls us to do battle for Him, He always goes before us. In God's grace, we are destined for victory in Jesus.**

We enter into that victory when we learn the lessons of preparation for victory. God does not call us to believe in ourselves or in our own adequacy. Rather, He strips us bare, taking us down to the point where we must depend on Him. Then, in grace, He takes us by the hand and teaches us that we can trust completely in Him. We need to learn the lesson of dependence so that we may move on to learn the lesson of confidence. We learn that we can do nothing without Him. Then we delight to discover that we can rely completely upon him. Having learned these great lessons, we are prepared for victory.

When Gideon's men are given instructions on how to attack, they must wonder how they are going to carry it out (vv. 16–18). Their weapons are trumpets and large clay pots containing torches. They are told to blow the trumpets, shatter the jars, brandish the torches, and shout. That's it! But even though they do not understand all that God is going to do, they choose to trust their leader, because they have become convinced that the Lord stands behind Gideon's strange plans.

There is a great lesson here: It is not our responsibility to understand how God is going to keep His Word or accomplish His work; our responsibility is to know what He calls us to do and to do it.

What does it mean to be prepared for battle in today's context? How can you submit to God's preparation?

Is God calling you to do something that you don't understand? What can you do to hang on to His command and promises?

Day 25

It is absurd to believe that 300 men could defeat 135,000 men with jars, torches, and horns. But they did, because God was with them. The noise, lights, and shouts by Gideon's men had their role, but the confusion among the Midianites was God-induced (Judges 7:22).

The tone of the passage, however, changes in Judges 8:1–3. God has given His people an astounding victory, but they allow petty tribal disputes to rob Him of His rightful glory and the people of their joy. Gideon had summoned help from the tribe of Ephraim, who seized the fords of the Jordan where the Midianites tried to cross to escape into the desert and captured two of their top commanders. But rather than rejoice that they had been allowed a part in God's great deliverance, they come to Gideon with a smouldering complaint (Judges 8:1) motivated by personal jealousy and injured pride. There is no joy or thanksgiving, only bitterness of heart and resentment.

In a time of victory, the greatest danger often comes from within the circle of God's professing people. They don't see what God is doing; all they can see is their own cause or convenience, and they view everything based on how it impacts their own interests.

Gideon's response is admirable. He could have chosen to put the Ephraimites in their place or defend himself, but he shrewdly minimises his role and maximises theirs (vv. 2–3). So what if he was wronged or criticised? It is more important for God's people to be united than for Gideon to be vindicated. How much better it is to take our hurts to the Lord and let Him deal with it, than to insist on our rights at the expense of dividing God's people.

But Gideon's response is also sad. While his diplomacy is successful, he focuses entirely on the horizontal. He doesn't insist on the credit for himself, but neither does he give it to the Lord, where it truly belongs. He doesn't direct the Ephraimites to God as the source of victory, nor does he make it clear that he had been acting under a divine commission.

There is nothing Satan loves more than to see Christians fighting with one another.

If we are fighting with each other, we are not pursuing the enemy. Satan can subvert our every effort by sowing disunity, leaving us so confused that we turn on our fellow believers. He loves to see us divided and draws us into having misplaced priorities, where we subtly substitute our cause for God's cause and thus pursue the wrong objectives or do the right thing for the wrong reasons. Disunity will always occur when our perspective is horizontal, not vertical.

Day 26

Things are beginning to take a dark turn. In the last two episodes of the military campaign, Gideon has made it personal. It has become about him, not about God and His glory, and that poison seeps into his actions.

We see it first in his retaliation against Succoth and Peniel. These towns certainly deserve Gideon's anger, as their behaviour is reprehensible (Judges 8:6, 8). The problem is that Gideon responds in a way that is out of proportion to their offence (vv. 16–17). The deliverer is acting like an oppressor because he has made himself the issue. We see it again in Gideon's pursuit of the Midianite kings (vv. 12, 18–21). This is about a personal vendetta—revenge for the death of his brothers—rather than for a national or spiritual cause. Gideon has reduced his God-given victory to a personal feud.

Gideon has come a long way, but now he is drifting quickly away from a focus on God and His agenda for Israel. God wanted to remind Israel that they owed their deliverance to Him alone (Judges 7:2), but Gideon is making it about himself. He has sown the seeds of compromise, and his people will reap a bitter harvest. Sometimes, the most dangerous time is after the battle, not before.

How quickly, too, does human nature forget that the victory is God's and try to take the credit for itself! Jeremiah 17:5 warns us not to trust in man or depend on the flesh for our strength. Yet that is exactly what we see happening among God's people. Out of the Israelites' spiritually ungrateful hearts, there arises an ungodly idea: they give Gideon credit he does not deserve, and offer him a kingship (v. 22).

This request was outside their prerogative. Israel was not a democracy, but a theocracy, with God as the king and the kingmaker. It was His prerogative to give His people a king when and if He pleased (Deuteronomy 17:14–20). Israel did not need a king; they had a King. Likewise, it is God's will for His church to be a theocracy. The New Testament church had elders and deacons who served as shepherds and leaders, but it had only one Head: the Lord Jesus Christ.

One of the oldest tendencies of our sinful hearts is to exalt others to the place that belongs only to God.

We must take care that, in our desire for truly biblical authority and dynamic

growth in our churches, we do not implicitly reject the teaching of the Word of God about church life.

ThinkThrough

How can we avoid side-lining God's purposes and pursuing our own agenda?

What principles of leadership can we learn from Jesus? How can we apply them in our own lives and in the church today? See Mark 10:42–45.

Day 27

Read Judges 8:24–28

Gideon's greatest triumph was followed by his greatest mistake. As a result, the final story of his life carries a mixed message—one of glorious moments, missed opportunities, and massive failure. The irony is that Gideon's decline began immediately after his affirmation of God's absolute kingship (Judges 8:23). Unfortunately, his actions were not consistent with his words. **It is never enough to declare the truth; we need to live it.**

We aren't told what motivates Gideon to turn the war booty into an ephod, a garment symbolising the office of the high priest (vv. 24–27). It may have been a desire to have a means to divine God's will, or some distorted idea that there is a spiritual vacuum he needs to fill. But he ends up creating an idolatrous cult that defies the Word of God. It may have been done in the name of Yahweh, but his act is spiritually disastrous: Israel prostitutes itself by worshipping it. The term "prostituted" always refers to spiritual unfaithfulness, the adultery of spiritual apostasy, to God.

God had commanded worship through the Levitical priesthood at the tabernacle, which was at Shiloh. Gideon's act—worshipping at Ophrah—was in direct violation of God's Word: he had no right to try to solve a genuine problem in his own way.

The essence of all compromise, and ultimately of all heresy, is that we believe that we have the right to alter or improve the revealed will of God. But anything less than complete obedience leads to spiritual disaster: we cannot improve on God's precepts. Good intentions are not more important than complete obedience; our need is not clever innovations, but consistent obedience to the Word of God.

This is a constant problem for believers in today's secular, amoral society. People around us live as an authority unto themselves, and we are at risk of adopting the same standard, doing what is right in our own eyes rather than ordering our lives around God's Word. But as society attacks the integrity of the Bible and tries to undermine its sufficiency, we must remember that God's Word is complete and absolutely authoritative. Nothing and no one must be allowed to take its place among God's people.

Unfortunately, the ephod episode was not an isolated one in Gideon's life. Even more evident is the effect on the next generation. By denying the complete authority of God's Word in his life, Gideon led his family down a path headed directly to apostasy. When we reject the authority of God's Word in any way, decline is inevitable.

Day 28

Read Judges 8:29–35

The Holy Spirit does not dwell upon this part of Gideon's biography. However, enough is said for us to realise what happened. The man who refused the throne adopts a very kingly lifestyle.

First, there is his "royal" harem (Judges 8:30). Occasionally, an ordinary Israelite might have more than one wife, but large-scale polygamy was practised only by rulers who could afford it. Gideon adopts not only the Canaanite idea of having a harem but apparently their moral standards as well, because he has a concubine in Shechem (v. 31). Gideon also lives in "royal" prosperity. He had begun his career as the "weakest in Manasseh" (Judges 6:15), but he ends his life in great luxury. This is exactly what God warned against in Deuteronomy 17:17. The final evidence of Gideon's backsliding is found in the name he gave his son—Abimelek ("My father is king", v. 31). The boy is claiming for his father what Gideon had apparently renounced in verse 23. Later on, chapter 9 reveals that his family receives the impression that the next king would come from among Gideon's sons. How far away Gideon's great victory is now!

The ending of Gideon's story is a sad one, but it has some important lessons for us today:

One, we cannot compromise our obedience to the Word of God, as Gideon did with God's commands. The path of partial obedience is the way to spiritual defeat, and the path of compromise means that the Lord will not be able to use our lives to make a permanent impact for Jesus Christ. We cannot alter God's Word, and we cannot choose to obey only what we deem appropriate. His Word must be supreme.

Two, the most glorious profession of the lordship of Jesus Christ must be followed by the consistent practice of that lordship (see 1 Corinthians 10:12). **The evidence of our dedication to the Lord must be worked out in our lives over the course of time.** Gideon professed the kingship of God over Israel in clear, unequivocal terms, but then he felt free to alter the King's clear commands. How has your dedication to the Lord altered your life? Is it only a glorious profession, or is it a habit of life? There is no substitute for hard-nosed, consistent obedience.

Three, the only safe place to keep our spiritual eyes is on the Lord Jesus. Even Gideons may backslide. The most spiritual Christian may fail. God the Holy Spirit calls us to run the race before us, looking away from all else to Jesus, the source and protector of our faith (Hebrews 12:1–2). He alone is our unfailing example.

Day 29

Read Judges 9:1–57

The lesson of Abimelek's story is simple but powerful: if we reject the true King, we will be ruled by a usurper. If the throne is not filled by God, it will be filled by an Abimelek. When there is a spiritual vacuum, Satan will rush in to fill it. This principle applies in our organisations, whether political or congregational. If we do not seek and follow leaders who direct us to the kingship of Christ, we will fall into the hands of someone with negative and destructive leadership.

Abimelek is a prototype of an abusive leader. He leads for his own benefit, uses power for selfish purposes, and hides his own agenda behind an altruistic one. He knows the insecurities and aspirations of his followers, and exploits them for his own ends (Judges 9:2–3).

But the problem is not just one of bad leadership—it is also one of evil "followership". When Abimelek executes 69 of his half-brothers, nobody raises a hand against him (vv. 5–6). In this one act, both Israel and Abimelek reveal themselves for what they are: Israel is an immoral society prepared to tolerate the most atrocious acts, while Abimelek is a ruthless man, prepared to use any means to gain his ends. People often get the leaders they deserve.

We need to develop an instinctive suspicion of anyone who usurps Christ's place in His church. There is a subtle temptation to give undue prominence to gifted people who boost our self-image and feed our baser instincts. We need to beware any tendency to minimise the character qualifications for leadership and the servant mindset, and to watch the workings of our own hearts.

So it is too in our lives. The flesh cannot rule where the Spirit is king. The Christian life is not about beating down the flesh and trying to keep our old nature in its place, but about enthroning Jesus in His proper place (Romans 6:16). **If Christ does not rule our lives, our sinful nature will.**

Jotham's fable (Judges 9:8–15) shows that if we turn from God's purposes to our own devices, our choices will be foolish and self-destructive. Too often, Christians do what the Shechemites did when they finally recognise their mistake. Instead of turning to God in repentance and submitting to Him as king, they try to deal with Abimelek on their own (v. 25).

If Christ is not King in word and deed, then a "thornbush" will seize control

(v. 15). This is true in our country, churches, and personal lives. We must beware all attempts to take the place that belongs only to Jesus. Whether we are followers or leaders, we must ensure that He alone is Lord.

Day 30

Read Judges 10:1–16

Unfortunately, not many of us realise the stupidity of sin or recognise it for what it is—spiritual insanity. The prodigal son left his father until, one day, watching pigs fill their bellies with corn husks, he came to his senses (Luke 15:17). That is the essence of repentance—a return to reality about ourselves.

Only when we see sin in that way can we appreciate the seriousness of Israel's apostasy. Judges 10:6 records the sixth time the Israelites turn their backs on the living God to worship pagan gods. This is one of the bleakest spiritual periods in the nation's history. There is virtually no pagan god, however depraved, that they will not pursue. So once again God turns them over to foreign invaders (vv. 7–8). When Israel finally reaches its breaking point and cries out to the Lord for relief, their words sound genuine (v. 10). But the Lord is anything but impressed. He treats their cry with contempt, considering it insincere and manipulative (vv. 11–14).

There is a great difference between regret and repentance. **Regret touches the emotions; repentance touches the will and involves a change of mind and intent.** Judas regretted what he had done (Matthew 27:3), but that didn't drive him to the Lord, only to despair. Regret is remorse over the consequences of an act; repentance involves recognition of our wrong relationship with God and re-ordering of our lives around Him. That is why many of us have never known God at work in our lives. Until we deal radically with our sin in the presence of God and fill our minds with His truth such that we act upon it, we will not know His power.

When the Lord's refusal to respond to their superficial regret drives the Israelites to examine their hearts more deeply, the result is true repentance (Judges 10:15). This time words come with appropriate actions (v. 16). Scholars are divided over whether God's response in verse 16 meant that He was annoyed with Israel, or that He was moved by His people's suffering. The fact remains, however, that God does not give up on His sinful people, no matter how persistently they rebel against Him. He persists in His grace towards them and finally says, "That is enough. I won't allow them to endure anymore."

Don't believe Satan's lie that the God of the Old Testament is a stern, unforgiving God who delights in judgment. He is a God of incessant love and infinite mercy. Again and again He displays these characteristics, and that is even more true on this side of the cross. He is the God of all grace.

Reflect on sin in your life. Do you recognise it for what it is?

How do you know whether your response is regretful or repentant?

Day 31

Read Judges 10:17–11:3

Many Christians suffer from an inferiority complex because they do not fit the mould of a godly servant, whatever they imagine it to be. Sometimes the fault is ours because we put restrictions on God; sometimes it is others', who believe they have the Lord figured out. Thank God, there is no such mould, no established pattern into which we must fit before He can use us. God can use each one of us.

Jephthah is a man with a tragic past, a checkered career, and more than his share of faults. His inner conflicts run deep. Yet God in His wisdom chooses to use and work through him. Let's look at his first two stages of development.

First, Jephthah is the man nobody wanted (Judges 11:1–3). His mother was a common prostitute, and he grew up on the margins of his family. When his father died, he was forced to flee and make his way in the world, all on his own. Alone, that is, except for God. The grace of God was at work in Jephthah's life, rescuing him from a hopeless future. God does not submit to human prejudices, and is not limited by social, parental, and environmental factors. We are not a prisoner of our past, no matter how difficult or dysfunctional. God delights in using the "unusable" and in making the "ugly" beautiful.

Second, Jephthah became the bandit chief (Judges 11:3). After he fled to the frontier area of Tob, he became the leader of a ragtag group, and it was there that he learnt leadership and warfare and strategy, which God later used for His glory. The practical skills he learnt in Tob became the reservoir on which he could draw when his role expanded. God does not ignore a person's strengths or skills, whether innate or acquired. He was overseeing Jephthah's development, long before he had any idea of his destiny. The years in the wilderness were not a waste, but an investment.

Sometimes, Christians fall into the trap of viewing their pre-conversion experience as a vast wasteland from which nothing can be redeemed. That is not true. The gifts and talents that you have can be used in some way for His glory and service. **God is sovereign both in your salvation and before it; nothing brought to Him is wasted.**

Jephthah did not have a father or mother to accept him, but he did have the Lord. He knew what it was to be taken in by the Lord when even those closest to him had rejected him, and because that rejection drew him closer to the Lord, it made Jephthah the man he was for God.

ThinkThrough

What kind of prejudice might we hold against others that could restrict their work for the Lord?

What past skills and experience do you have that could be used for God's glory? Ask Him for wisdom and guidance to put them to good use.

Day 32

Read Judges 11:4–11

When Jephthah is approached by the leaders of the people who had earlier rejected him to be the commander of the Israelite forces, there must have been a huge sense of vindication. But he is not too flattered to miss the fact that they had only offered him the position of "commander" (Judges 11: 6). Besides, he is still too angry and bitter about the way they had treated him to simply jump at the opportunity (v. 7).

There is an opportunistic streak in Jephthah, and he is fully prepared to take advantage of the situation for his purposes. He pushes for more (v. 9), and by the time the conversation ends, the elders have offered him the position of "head", both political and military leader (v. 10). It marks the third stage of Jephthah's development—from outlaw to leader. But although we are told that Jephthah enters into this role "before the LORD at Mizpah" (v. 11), it appears that this is nothing more than religious ceremonialism. Once again, the pattern repeats itself: the Lord is left out of their decisions. Nonetheless, God's sovereign plan will be fulfilled.

There is something to be learnt, however, from Jephthah's emergence (though perhaps not from his demands). This was not a position for which he had applied or worked, or to which he aspired. But, in God's own time, a door opened, and Jephthah was elevated to the position God had purposed for him.

Similarly, we do not need to create opportunities for service on our own; it is God's job to open doors. Our responsibility is to be fully involved and invested in the place where we find ourselves, doing the will of God wherever He has placed us and learning the lessons He is teaching us.

As a young man, preacher and writer, Charles Spurgeon was pondering his future after he lost a valuable opportunity to enter a prestigious university as a result of someone else's mistake. Deeply discouraged, he was replaying the events through his mind when he sensed the Holy Spirit telling him: "Should you then seek great things for yourself? Do not seek them" (Jeremiah 45:5).

"At that moment," he said, "I realised I would never go to Cambridge, and I would never amount to anything more than preaching to a congregation of 200 people." He committed himself to doing God's will, and six months later, through an unexpected chain of events, the 19-year-old found himself pastoring and preaching to 2,500 people every Sunday in London. That happened because he was willing to allow God to open doors in his life and to be faithful wherever he was at the time.

Live enthusiastically for God in the present, and He will concern himself with your future.

Day 33

The fourth stage of Jephthah's career puts him in a very different role. The illegitimate outcast and desert gang leader is now negotiating with an enemy king. A few days have brought him a very long way!

Jephthah is not a tentative leader. He is a fighting man, and we might expect him to strike first and ask questions later. Yet that is not the route he chooses to go. Before he draws up battle lines, Jephthah sends messengers to the king of Ammon asking the obvious question, "Why are you invading us?" (Judges 11:12, paraphrased). Ammon, however, counters with a claim that Israel had stolen Ammon's land earlier and that he is simply asserting his rightful claim over the land (v. 13).

Jephthah turns out to be a forceful and strong-minded negotiator who displays a strong grasp of historical realities. Convinced that the story of Israel is a story of what God has done, he gets straight to the point. "Check your history," he is in effect saying, "We captured the land from Sihon, the king of the Amorites, not the Ammonites" (vv. 15–22).

"Next, check your theology. The Lord God of Israel gave us this land, and we cannot surrender His gift. Go back and live in the land your god Chemosh has given you" (vv. 23–25, paraphrased). At this point Jephthah makes two mistakes. The first is that Chemosh was the god of the Moabites, not of the Ammonites, who worshipped Milcom. More seriously, he seems to be reducing Yahweh to just another god among many by his argument that Chemosh had given them their land while Israel's God had given His people theirs. This is a huge mistake and shows how much paganism has corrupted his thinking.

"Finally, check your logic. For 300 years we have held the land, and you have done nothing to recapture it. You can't start reclaiming it now! (vv. 26–27, paraphrased).

The significant thing is that Jephthah's answer is grounded in the truths of history. He does not argue about probability or dispute possibility, but merely stands firmly on fact. That is where a Christian should always stand. **The early Christians did not set their world aflame by expressing opinions or exchanging experiences, but by insisting upon the truth of who Jesus is and what He did.**

Our calling is the same. We do not go into the world merely telling people of our experience, but proclaiming Jesus Christ, telling people who He is, what He has done, and what He requires of us.

Day 34

Jephthah's vow (Judges 11:30–31) may have been the prayer of a sincere heart, zealous before God, but it was totally wrong. His ultimate problem was the ignorance of God's Word. Zeal without truth is dangerous, and dedication without biblical understanding produces fanaticism that destroys.

We have seen Jephthah negotiating with various groups, and now we see him trying to strike a bargain with God. For the promise of victory, he vows to sacrifice the first living thing that emerges from his house when he returns from battle. This is an attempt to manipulate God, and is a long way from the prayer of faith. Although Scripture does not specify what living thing Jephthah was offering, most scholars agree that he meant a human sacrifice. This betrays the extent to which Israel had assimilated Canaanite beliefs. Such sacrifices are prohibited in God's Word, and the practice is utterly pagan. Jephthah's vow, made in a time of apostasy and ignorance, is a hideous vow that contradicts the clear teaching of God's Word.

Jephthah's sincerity was destructive because he had a false view of God. He believed that God had to be bargained with and bribed. He could have claimed God's promises and rested in His grace, but he thought he could buy God's help with a human life. He also believed that God was sadistic and delighted in making His people unhappy. And he feared that God might abandon him halfway through the job, despite being empowered by the Holy Spirit (v. 29).

Many Christians falsely perceive God in the same way. They believe God is stern, sadistic, and legalistic; that He delights in the unpleasant and must be bargained with; that His favour must be earned; and that His presence cannot be counted on. But that is not the God of the Bible. When God gave Israel a stunning victory (vv. 32–33), His blessing was not the product of Jephthah's bargaining, but the gift of His grace.

There is one positive feature of Jephthah's action (vv. 35, 39) that challenges us today: despite the agonising personal cost— sacrificing his only child—he took his commitment seriously. How often do we make pledges to God that we do not honour?

Yet there were other options. Leviticus 27 explains that when a person is committed to the Lord, his life could be redeemed by the payment of a certain amount of money. If only Jephthah had known God's Word, he could have paid the ransom price and spared her. While there is some disagreement over what happened to her, it is most likely that she was sacrificed.

Ignorance of God's Word not only robs us of many of God's blessings, but can also have tragic consequences. Enormous evils have resulted because men and women have not understood the character of God as revealed in Scripture. Faith needs to be both sincere and understanding.

ThinkThrough

Think about your perceptions of God. How do they compare with what the Bible says about Him?

How can we correct other people's false perceptions of God in an encouraging, non-confrontational way?

Day 35

Read Judges 12:1–4

It is hard to imagine a more obnoxious attitude than that displayed by the Ephraimites. They had reacted to Gideon in a similar way in the middle of his battle with Midian (Judges 8:1). Ephraim was always brave after the battle.

The Ephraimites are arrogant, critical, envious, and self-important. They are sure of their own rights but unwilling to accept their responsibilities. For 18 years they have done nothing to resist Ammon themselves. But now they come with petty complaints and outrageous threats (v. 1). They seem always ready to fight with their brothers, but never against the enemy. But Jephthah is not Gideon. At first he points out that he had in fact called them, and they had not come (vv. 2–3). But when the Ephraimites will not listen to logic or truth, he and his men can contain their anger no longer, and turn in fury (v. 4).

It is important to realise the kind of ignorance the Ephraimites represent. It was an ignorance of their God-given responsibility. They were happy gathering up the spoil and quick to defend their rights and privileges, but they had no taste for battle. God had called them to join in the fight against the people on the land, but Ephraim was only willing to stand back and criticise until the battle was won.

It is easy to slip into becoming an Ephraimite when it comes to understanding our God-given responsibilities. Are we more than willing to let other believers move out into the world, confront others with the gospel, get involved in Sunday school, do menial work, go out to the mission field, and engage in Christian service? Do we reserve the right to criticise from the sidelines, and even to condemn what they do? Are we critical of our brothers and sisters who are involved in confronting the enemy, but not ourselves? Does our prayer go something like this: "Lord, use me in your work, but only in an advisory capacity!"?

The story is told of the man who came up to evangelist D. L. Moody and said, "Mr. Moody, I don't like the way you preach the gospel." Moody said, "You know, I'm always willing to learn. Tell me about the method you use." The man replied, "I guess I don't really have one."

"I'll tell you what," Moody said, "I like the way I do it better than the way you don't do it."

Let us beware the danger of becoming armchair generals; the church of Jesus Christ needs believers who are willing to take on their God-given responsibility to serve God and other believers. **Let us not complain and criticise. Instead, let us lead by example, encouragement, and edification!**

How can we avoid behaving like the Ephraimites? What are some signs that we can look out for?

How can you help others overcome this common tendency?

Day 36

The Ephraimites richly deserve to be taught a lesson. But in the midst of that lesson, Jephthah once again shows his ignorance of God's will and God's way. When the defeated Ephraimites attempt to flee across the Jordan, Jephthah and his men seize the crossings and test each traveller. Apparently, the Ephraimites' dialect did not use the "sh" sound. So whenever a man comes along who cannot say "Shibboleth", Jephthah's men put him to death. By the end of the battle, 42,000 Ephraimites are dead (Judges 12:5–6).

Those numbers are staggering. In one event Jephthah kills more of his fellow Israelites than all the judges combined killed of the enemy, with the exception of Gideon's destruction of the Midianites. Israel has become its own worst enemy.

Do you see the problem? Jephthah treated his fellow Israelites as if they were Ammonites. It is one thing to be provoked to battle, but it is quite another thing to cold-bloodedly execute Ephraimites. Jephthah was a hard-headed legalist; he could not tolerate the Ephraimites' unjustified provocation. He had experienced God's grace in his own life, but did not practise it in his relations with others. He knew nothing of the tenderness, love, and grace of God.

Jephthah is not alone, unfortunately. Church history contains many examples of Christians, including well-known leaders, falling out over differences with other believers and treating fellow believers as if they were enemies of the gospel.

Legalism is a deadly thing, and, more than that, it is a disaster. Jephthah's view of God appeared to be that He was a stern, unhappy judge who robbed life of joy. There is a great danger of Christians getting bound up in the ignorance of legalism. An old hymn based on Psalm 100 originally included the lines, "Sing to the LORD with cheerful voice, Him serve with mirth". Now that is beautifully biblical and faithful to what the psalmist wrote. But it was viewed as flippant and later changed to "Him serve with fear". Of course reverence has its place in worship, but so does mirth, and how sad it is that a distorted view of God resulted in a change to a beautiful hymn.

Jephthah had so much in his favour, but produced little lasting positive influence because of his ignorance. He did not adequately know the Word of God or the God of the Word, and he, his daughter, and his nation paid a high price for it. **There is no substitute for the knowledge**

of God that comes through the study of His Word.

ThinkThrough

Do you see evidence of legalism in your own life? Ask God for humility and wisdom to recognise, acknowledge, and address it.

What does the Bible say about God's character? See 1 John 4:8; Psalm 30:5; Exodus 34:6–7.

Day 37

Read Judges 13:1–25

Once again the Israelites did evil in the eyes of the Lord, and He delivers them into the hands of the Philistines for 40 years (Judges 13:1). The Philistines' two main weapons were trade and intermarriage. They were slowly choking the Israelites by compromise and assimilation. Israel was not being enslaved by military dominance but by spiritual and cultural seduction. Samson was the one person of his day who realised that a person or nation could not compromise and remain free to serve God.

Samson was a unique man for a unique time. He was to be a Nazirite, dedicated to God in a specific way (vv. 3–5; see Numbers 6:1–21). "Nazir" in Hebrew means "to set apart" or "to separate". He was sovereignly raised up by God for a definite purpose—delivering Israel from the Philistines (Judges 13:5).

We face a similar challenge today. Jesus also calls us to a specific purpose: to live in the world for His glory, as the salt of the earth and light of the world (see Matthew 5:13–14). He calls us to be "holy"—which means "set apart" or "distinct". But how do we put those two essentials together—in the world but separated from it; involved in the world but not conforming to it? What does it mean for a Christ-follower to live a separated life?

Samson's story offers us a lesson, carved in flesh, about some great truths on separation and holiness:

One, separation is meant to be a positive dedication to the Lord. Samson, however, saw his separation merely as legalistic, following a set of rules of dos and don'ts. In his heart, he was not dedicated to God. Some Christians understand holiness the same way, believing that it means living by a strict code of conduct. This can lead to isolationism or joyless asceticism. But that is not what God wants: separation is to be in a positive, joyful relationship with Jesus Christ.

Two, strength comes from separation. Not one Hebrew lifted a finger against the Philistines; they had been assimilated, compromised, and integrated. It is not easy to live in the world and avoid becoming like it, but that is exactly what God calls us to do. It was the separated Samson who had strength to fight.

Three, separation is always accompanied by enablement. God gave Samson the Holy Spirit to carry out His purpose. And He gives us His Spirit to enable us to live distinctively for Him in the world.

Four, Jesus gives us the model for separation. He spent time with and ministered to sinners, but did not do all that they did. He was separated from the world in His character, and never compromised, sinned, or accepted human values. To be separated from the world is to relate to it as Christ did (see John 17:5–17). We do not leave the world; we live in it for Him.

A separated Christian is a Bible-centred, Christ-controlled Christian, in whom God is reproducing His character by the Holy Spirit.

Day 38

We who are in Christ have enormous resources. We are infinitely blessed (see Ephesians 1:3; 1 Corinthians 1:30; Colossians 2:9–10). But we can squander those resources if, like Samson, we do not learn one vital lesson—the lesson of self-discipline and wholehearted commitment to the Lord.

Samson was a feared strongman with great potential. But he never learned to control himself (Judges 14:1–4). As a result, he squandered the resources God had given him, failed to accomplish his mission, was reduced to complete weakness, and died, having fallen short.

We first meet him in Timnah, where we see a man dominated by his appetites and desires (vv. 1–2). He sought to marry a Canaanite woman, which God clearly prohibits (Deuteronomy 7:3–4). But Samson went ahead regardless. This represents not only a betrayal of his calling but also direct disobedience to God himself. When questioned by his parents, his abrupt reply was: "She is right in my eyes" (v. 3, ESV). This says a great deal about him:

First, he was a man who rejected authority. Marrying the Canaanite woman was not only contrary to God's clearly-declared will, but also against the wishes of his parents. The principle of his life was: If I want to do it, I am going to do it.

Second, the basis of his behaviour was secular and selfish. The phrase, "Everyone did as he saw fit" (literally "what was right in his own eyes", Judges 17:6; 21:25), is used twice to account for the spiritual chaos and catastrophe during this period of Israel's history. Samson was a spiritual anarchist who had adopted the social values of his pagan contemporaries.

We live in a period of moral, spiritual, and ethical anarchy. But what is especially sad is when believers adopt the world's approach to life. Ultimately, it comes down to whether we are going to live by God's authority or by our own standards. The great battleground of our time is the battleground of authority.

Samson was an undisciplined man who indulged himself freely, controlled by his passions. He saw no reason to curb his desires. Today, sexual immorality is a common reason why Christians lose their effectiveness for Jesus Christ. But there are many other problem areas.

Paul understood the danger of the lack of self-control. He disciplined his body so that he would be mastered by Christ (1 Corinthians 9:27). Almost anything can distract us from focusing on Jesus—things that may be beautiful and good in their proper place, but can cause damage when self-discipline breaks down. **Self-discipline is not denying our drives and desires; it is submitting them to God's will and timing.** If we do not discipline our lives, we can squander our resources and lose our effectiveness.

Day 39

Samson is a man who is a law unto himself, who believes that he is the exception to any rule. In that way, he is a living illustration of the spiritual anarchy of his people, and that attitude will bring him to a premature death. All through this chapter, he toys with the vows that set him apart.

First, along the way to Timnah, he becomes separated from his parents and finds himself in a vineyard (Judges 14:5). That should have raised an alarm, since a Nazirite was to abstain from anything that comes from the grapevine (see Numbers 6:1–4). There, he meets a lion and tears it apart (Judges 14:6). But he chooses not to tell his parents about it. Why the secrecy? Was it because killing violated the Nazirite prohibition on contact with the dead (see Numbers 6:6–7)?

On a return trip, he intentionally visits the scene of his battle with the lion. This is a blatant breach of his vow to avoid contact with the dead, further compounded when he eats the honey from the carcass (Judges 14:8–9). At his marriage to the Canaanite woman, he throws a seven-day feast—a drinking party (v. 10). While such feasts were customary, we could ask: why would a Nazirite host a party serving wine from the vineyard?

The only positive thing to be said for Samson in this entire episode is that he honours the bet on his riddle, although in a brutal way (vv. 12–17, 19). What is unexpected is that the power to do this is attributed to the Holy Spirit, who "came powerfully upon him" (v. 19). Whatever we make of the morality of Samson's actions, we see in verse 4 that God is at work in all these things to bring about the deliverance of His people.

The Lord did not direct Samson into disobedience or immoral actions. But He was at work through Samson, accomplishing His plans through this very unworthy instrument. We cannot escape responsibility or accountability for our sins, but in the providential purpose of God, it is His intentions that triumph.

A few years after Samson's death, another man became the judge of Israel. Like Samson, he was born under a vow. But while Samson neither liberated his people nor turned their hearts to God, Samuel changed the course of Israel's history. Every area of life in Israel was touched for good through the life and ministry of Samuel. What was the difference? It is found in 1 Samuel 15:22, in Samuel's words: "Does the Lord delight in burnt offerings and sacrifices as much as in obeying the Lord? To obey is better than sacrifice, and to heed is better than the fat of rams."

Samson may have fulfilled God's purpose, but sadly, he never understood obedience to God.

ThinkThrough

Why do you think God prefers obedience to sacrifice?

How can you live a life of consistent commitment to God's authority and self-discipline that brings all of your life under the lordship of Jesus Christ?

Day 40

Read Judges 15:1–17

Samson was a man with a passion for freedom in the middle of a society committed to compromise. Fellow Israelites were committed to appeasement, but Samson recognised that there could be no compromise with the enemy. Yet the way he conducted that battle missed the point. It was supposed to be a God-given mission, not a personal vendetta. One of the terrible things about violence as a method is that when we get on the treadmill of personal revenge and retaliation, it becomes very hard to get off (Judges 15:3–5, 7–8).

Indeed, Samson's battles were always about himself, about revenge for perceived mistreatment. Although his calling was to begin Israel's deliverance (see Judges 13:5), he never put the cause of his nation or God first. He was a deliverer who never led his people out in battle, a leader who never fought for God's honour, and an agent of God who never publicly gave praise to the Lord (Judges 15:14–16).

There is also something striking about the spiritual condition of the Judeans. When the Philistines invade Judah to capture Samson, they meet no resistance (v. 9). Three things stand out:

First, the Israelites have become thoroughly accommodated to the spiritual status quo (v. 11). We see this in Judah giving up a great opportunity to be free from the Philistines. They have a leader of amazing strength, an army of 3,000 men (v. 11), and a God who promises victory. They could have rallied around Samson's leadership, but they have become so degraded by compromise that they accuse him of being a troublemaker. They have made peace in their hearts with defeat. **It is possible for believers to get to a point where they prefer slavery to freedom, where compromise is more comfortable than commitment to God's calling**. We do not believe things will change, so we accept our situation and give up the fight. Or we are hindered in our growth by other Christians accustomed to an anaemic, wishy-washy spiritual life.

Second, those who compromised are ignored by the enemy (v. 10). The Philistines have no quarrel with the Judeans because they present no threat. Only when a Christ-follower commits to serving God wholeheartedly and battling on the front lines does Satan work hard to side-track him. If you are encountering opposition in your life, thank God—it shows that you are making Satan take notice.

Third, compromised people do the enemy's work for them (v. 12). The men of Judah are so defeatist in their mind-set that they offer to capture Samson themselves. There are no non-combatants or neutral parties in spiritual warfare. If we are not actively involved in a positive way for the Lord, we can become positive hindrances to the cause of Christ.

How can we avoid turning God's mission into a personal battle?

In what ways can we become used to the spiritual status quo of today? Have we made peace with defeat?

Day 41

In today's passage, we find Samson exhausted after the battle. With the fight over, he can finally think about his physical needs, and we hear him pray—for the first time (Judges 15:18). But, like everything else about him, it is a curious mixture of faith and self-centred complaint. There are several lessons we can learn:

One, taking our enemies seriously: At first, Samson confesses that his victory is, in fact, God's victory ("You have given", v. 18). He knows that his power is due to God's intervention, and declares himself to be "your servant". He also sees the enemy for what they are ("the uncircumcised"), and is fully aware of the dangers they represent. **Likewise, Christians today need to be aware that they have three enemies—the world, the flesh, and the devil—that are committed to keeping them from living a spiritual life.** Like Samson, until we take these enemies seriously, we cannot overcome them.

Two, not blaming God for our own choices: Samson's prayer turns quickly into a complaint ("Must I now die", v. 18). Ironically, he is in such a situation because of his own actions—the fire in the fields and the revenge on the murderers of his wife had been his idea, not God's (vv. 3–8). How often we too complain to God about things that are the result of our own foolish choices!

Three, victory often makes us vulnerable to a let-down: We must be careful not to lose fellowship with the Lord in the middle of victory. We also need to learn to protect ourselves against the inevitable let-down that follows great emotional experiences.

Four, the importance of physical needs: Note also the close connection between our physical and spiritual condition. What Samson needed was not a Bible conference, but a drink of water. We often ignore simple facts about our spiritual condition, and neglect to look after our bodies. An improper diet, lack of sleep, poor physical conditioning, illness—all these can affect us spiritually.

Yet God in His grace answered Samson's prayer. First, He supplies water (v. 19). Samson, however, again directs attention to the wrong place: the spring is called "En Hakkore", or "Spring of the Caller"—it memorialises the one who prays, rather than the God who answers. Second, the Lord establishes Samson's judgeship (v. 20), using him to lead and guide His people in a limited way.

Flawed as he was, Samson did what no one else did—loosening the Philistine's chokehold on his people. But it's sad to think of how much more he might have accomplished had he not kept missing the point, always perceiving his circumstances to be about himself, and not about his God.

ThinkThrough

What are the dangers posed by our spiritual enemies? How can we take them seriously?

How can we avoid Samson's mistake of thinking that circumstances are all about ourselves?

Day 42

Read Judges 16:1–14

With its blend of love, sex, violence, and treachery, the story of Samson's downfall at Delilah's hands is one of the Bible's best-known stories. Yet it is not unique: countless Christians have lost their spiritual strength for exactly the same reasons.

Samson did not fail because the temptation was too strong or inescapable. He failed because he toyed and trifled with sin, even seeking it out in Gaza, a stronghold of the Philistines (Judges 16:1), where he deliberately exposed himself to the enemy. His carnal self-confidence, an immature belief in his invincibility, made him pliable dough in the hands of Delilah. Overconfidence in self blinds us to reality (see Proverbs 16:18; 1 Corinthians 10:12). Three important principles about temptation, as represented in Delilah, lie at the heart of why we succumb:

One, moral compromise always makes us vulnerable. If Samson had not had a sinful relationship with Delilah—there is no suggestion that they were married—he would never have been open to this temptation. In our lives, the compromise is often more subtle. It lies in the material we read, the programs we watch, and the values we accept. We do not fall off a cliff morally; we go down a slope, speeding up until we cannot stop.

That is why personal purity is such a crucial issue. To compromise, even in our thoughts, makes us vulnerable.

Two, temptation comes to us in attractive packages. Delilah was a beautiful, attractive woman. **When sin comes, it will not come as something ugly and destructive, but as something that presents itself as desirable, good, and fulfilling.**

Three, temptation comes when we choose the wrong company. Samson's choice of the wrong kind of girls—the Philistine woman from Timnah, the prostitute from Gaza, and Delilah—helped to destroy his character. God is not calling us to an isolationism that retreats into a holy huddle. But we need to look carefully at our friendships to discover whether those associations are drawing us away from Jesus (see 1 Corinthians 15:33). Some of us will never grow up in Christ until we break off those relationships that are dragging us down.

When we toy with temptation, it traps us. The New Testament does not ask us to fight this kind of temptation; it tells us to run away from it (1 Corinthians 6:18; 10:14; 1 Timothy 6:11; 2 Timothy 2:22).

There may be things in our lives that we need to deal with, or major areas that need to be changed if we are going to preserve our character. It could include our lifestyles, leisure activities, or even our jobs. Temptation is a constant part of the Christian life. Fleeing is hard, but it is essential.

Day 43

Aren't you struck by the sheer foolishness of Samson? Despite all the evidences of Delilah's betrayal, he blurts out the most precious secret of his life to a woman who is committed to his destruction (Judges 16:17). And how can he go to sleep in her lap (v. 19) after what she has done—betray his secret three times (vv. 9, 12, 14)—and what he has now revealed (v. 17)? Surely he must know what she is going to do. What fools sin makes of us!

In light of the way he has lived, it is striking to realise that Samson is completely aware of his calling as a Nazirite. Whatever his problem is, it isn't ignorance—he knows the terms of his strength (v. 17). For 40 years, Samson has kept one part of his vow. He has broken all the other parts, but he has kept his hair uncut. There is no magic in his hair; it is only a symbol of his commitment to God. But when his hair is shaved, Samson's feeble dedication crumbles completely (v. 19).

In verse 21, we see the awful results of Samson's sin. This was the mighty man who had stalked off with the gates of Gaza in an amazing display of physical strength (v. 3). Now he is bound, humiliated, and blind. There is irony here. It was his eyes that had constantly gotten him into trouble. He had been morally and spiritually blind, and now he is physically blind.

God had not failed Samson; it was Samson's pride and self-indulgence that had destroyed his life. With all of our potential, strength, and accomplishments, we can end up like Samson if we do not learn the danger of toying with temptation.

But even when Samson is in prison, a total failure, God does not abandon him. Verse 22 is a bright beacon of hope in a very dark place: "But the hair on his head began to grow again after it had been shaved." **Even in the midst of the worst kind of failure, God is present, working to restore Samson.** God refuses to give up on him.

It may be that you know all too well what it is like to fail just as Samson failed. You have fallen to temptation, and you would be ashamed if anyone knew about it. There is a bumper sticker that puts it beautifully: "Christians aren't perfect; they're forgiven." The hair can grow again. God can use you again—even in your failure, He will not abandon you. When you fail, come to God, claim His forgiveness, and He will work His healing grace in your life.

How can we avoid Samson's mistake of toying with temptation?

How has God worked His healing grace in your life after past mistakes? Recall those times and thank God for His forgiveness and grace.

Day 44

Read Judges 16:23–28

Hebrews 11, "God's Hall of Faith", could well be entitled "God's Hall of Reclaimed Failures". There is scarcely an individual without a serious blemish. But God is in the business of restoring failures. The spiritually successful Christian is not the person who never fails, but the believer who learns how to accept God's remedy for failure. No matter how far we fall, we never fall beyond the possibility of His forgiveness (1 John 1:9). But we need to learn from what we have done wrong and lay hold of the forgiveness of God. If we wallow in guilt, turn to self-pity, or make excuses, we will be overwhelmed by our failure.

Samson had never learned from his failures, but now, he is learning the reality of God's discipline in his life (see Hebrews 12:6–9). Sometimes, God must strip away everything that keeps us from trusting in Him. It may be a very painful process, but His purpose is not to destroy us; it is to build us up and teach us to trust in Him. **God's discipline, designed to produce maturity and restore us to usefulness, is never isolated from His restoration.**

But while forgiveness is immediate, restoration is gradual; it takes time for Samson's hair to grow. When a significant failure occurs in our lives, it is nearly always the result of sinful habits, accumulated over years of disobedience. Those habits must be unlearned and replaced by new ones, and that process takes time. We must also face the fact that God does not automatically erase the past; Samson does not receive new eyes. We must not minimise the seriousness of sin and its consequences. On the other hand, we must not miss the reality of God's forgiveness. He is able to turn the consequences of our sin into instruments for His glory.

Judges 16:28 gives us an insight into Samson's heart. It is a prayer of faith from a man who has been through God's refining fire. He has accepted God's forgiveness, has become totally dependent on Him, and is now committed to God. Having undergone the discipline of God, Samson is a new man, trusting in God and deriving his strength from God rather than from himself. Now his strength is disciplined by faith—but it took failure to teach him this response.

One of the hardest things to do is to accept forgiveness. We keep digging up the past, replaying our sins for every last ounce of guilt. But the cross repairs the irreparable and forgives the unforgivable. Our sin has been forgiven and dealt with for all eternity. Do not keep remembering and replaying your sin.

ThinkThrough

Are you undergoing God's discipline today? Ask Him for a heart to learn from your failure so that you can be restored for His glory.

How do you know you are forgiven? See 1 John 1:9.

Day 45

Summoned to the pagan temple for his enemies' entertainment, Samson asks to be allowed to rest against the pillars. If he had his sight, the Philistines would never have allowed him anywhere near those pillars (Judges 16:26). But nobody is worried about Samson. After all, he is an ordinary blind man, no threat to anyone. He is a failure. The grace of God takes the very results of Samson's failure and uses his apparent weakness and blindness to win a great victory. Because Samson is prepared to trust God even though he had failed, the Lord answers his prayer (v. 28) in a supernatural way. Samson becomes a living embodiment of the truth that God is a God of grace. Restoration is not based on performance, yet Satan tempts us to believe that it is—we convince ourselves that we must earn God's favour, that we have to achieve something before He will love and use us.

When Samson had physical capacity, he was proven to be a miserable failure. Now, in his distress, he calls on the Lord (v. 28), and the Lord meets his need. God can use blinded, broken, forgiven sinners. He can even use the blindness that is the product of our failures. This is a truth we need for our lives on a daily basis.

The results of Samson's prayer are spectacular (v. 30). In some ways, verse 30 is sad—it is a reminder of the tragic way in which Samson traded God-given power and potential for a carnal pursuit of pleasure. If only he had followed the Lord with all his heart, how much more he could have done! At the same time, however, verse 30 is also full of the grace of God. Samson's death is not a defeat; it is a victory. The failure dies a hero.

By God's grace, failure, when properly dealt with, can be a giant step forward in our growth to becoming like Christ. **We have a God who restores failures.** The hair can grow again. Are you a failure? Of course you are—there is no such thing as a perfect Christian.

How can we deal with failure? First, we need to admit it and see ourselves for what we are—blind, shaven, and chained. Second, we need to accept God's forgiveness. 1 John 1:9 is a truth to be lived. Third, we need to be patient. Restoration takes time; the Lord wants to build habits in our lives that will enable us to become godly Christians (Psalm 119:67) and keep us in the Word. Fourth, we need to trust God to use us. We can ask Him to show us how even the scars left by our sin can become instruments to display His glory. He will!

ThinkThrough

What are some ways in which we might depend on our performance rather than on God's grace for our restoration?

How can we encourage others when they have failed?

Day 46

Read Judges 17:1–6

As we come to the end of Judges, we find an epilogue of two parts, joined by a common theme that rings throughout the entire book: people doing "what was right in [their] own eyes" (Judges 17:6; 21:25, NKJV). The first part (chapters 17–18) depicts the spiritual anarchy of a rebellious nation, while the second (chapters 19–21) shows their moral anarchy. Both parts focus on the fate of a tribe (Dan in chapters 17–18; Benjamin in chapters 19–21), and the emphasis is on ordinary people, not tribal leaders or judges.

In chapter 17, we are introduced to a new character, Micah. Right from the start, his story is pathetic.

Micah means "who is like the Lord", but his name is a total contradiction to his character and actions. Micah begins as a thief (v. 2), and advances to become an idolater (v. 5). The house of God was at Shiloh (see Judges 18:31), but Micah establishes a full-fledged shrine in his home, complete with a priestly garment, a molten image (an idol of poured silver), a graven image (a carved idol coated with silver), and a number of household gods. Then he installs one of his sons—a non-Levite—as priest.

Micah had invented his own little religion in the hills of Ephraim, not far from Shiloh. His idolatry had nothing to do with the unavailability of God's house; it had everything to do with his refusal to follow God's Word. It was an act of spiritual anarchy (Judges 17:6). It is important to note that Micah was not worshipping Baal or a false god. He was trying to worship the true God with his idols. He says: "Now I know that the LORD [Yahweh] will be good to me" (v. 13).

God forbids the worship not only of false gods, but also of the true God by images (see Exodus 20:4). Such false worship robs God of His glory: no picture or image can properly honour Him, and no created likeness can possibly reflect His nature. In fact, such images hide and deface His majesty and greatness. That is why God detests images. They mislead people and give false views of God—and nothing is more destructive than that.

But our greater problem is mental idols. While we may not build physical idols like Micah did, we may form mental pictures of God, saying things like, "I like to think of God as the great Father in the skies, not as a judge." But God is who He is and what He is; human concepts of God are irrelevant. **God has revealed himself, and He demands that our understanding of Him**

conform to what He has revealed about himself in His Word.

What mental images of God do you hold? Who or what shapes your view of God?

What can we do to ensure that we have an accurate view of God?

Day 47

We now meet Micah's new "legitimate" priest, a wandering Levite. One phrase tells us a great deal about him: "[He] departed . . . from Bethlehem in Judah, to stay wherever he might find a place" (Judges 17:8, NASB). In other words, he was looking for a place to better himself. That was a perfectly natural ambition, except that in this case, it was totally contrary to the will of God. Levites were men dedicated to God's service. They were not to be opportunists moving from place to place, looking for a job. They had been assigned specific cities in which to live and serve God (Numbers 18:1–2; Joshua 21). This was a man who refused to be satisfied with God's arrangements for his life. Instead of living faithfully within the sphere of his divine calling, he was committed to self-promotion and to personal betterment.

One of Satan's most subtle tricks is causing Christians to become dissatisfied with the life circumstances and the area of service God has given them. "I should be better known." "I should be paid more." "I should receive more praise." Far too often, Christians will not do a job because they think it is beneath them. Or they will leave a church because no one pays enough attention to them. Or they will pout because someone else is more important than they are.

The next stage in the Levite's career occurs when he becomes Micah's priest—not God's (Judges 17:10–11). Once again there is a direct denial of God's Word (see Numbers 16:1–35). Later, he will get a promotion when the tribe of Dan makes him an offer he cannot refuse (Judges 18:19–20). The self-promoting upward mobility of the priest will take him deeper into apostasy and sin. He had begun as a disaffected individual, and he will become the apostate priest responsible for leading an entire tribe into idolatry.

It is a sobering moment when we finally learn the identity of the Levite— "Jonathan son of Gershom, the son of Moses" (Judges 18:30). This upwardly mobile, utterly corrupt, make-up-your-own-religion Levite could trace his ancestry back to the very one through whom God's law had been given! It is a stark reminder that it is no good having a godly ancestor if you do not know God yourself. Godliness is not genetic.

The lesson of Jonathan's life is the necessity of godly contentment with God's arrangements for our lives. What is your attitude towards service for Jesus Christ? Are you looking for a place, or are you seeking God's place? Are you content to be what and where

God wants you to be? Or are you a Jonathan, climbing the ladder of Christian promotion, wanting prominence, attention, and praise?

ThinkThrough

How might we develop a professional attitude toward the Lord's work, even if we are not in vocational Christian work?

How can we learn to be content with God's arrangements for our lives? See 1 Timothy 6:6.

Day 48

Read Judges 18:1–31

When we read in Judges 18:1 that the tribe of Dan "had not yet come into an inheritance", we are not to think that God had failed them, or that Dan had been omitted when Joshua divided up the land. Joshua 19:40–48 makes it clear that their assigned portion was between Ephraim and Judah. But Dan had refused to trust God by driving out the Amorites, and as a result were forced into the hills and reduced to living in two towns (Judges 1:34). The tribe was left with two choices: repent of their unbelief and trust God to keep His Word as they entered into battle against their enemies, or look for a comfortable place where the natives were vulnerable to a sneak attack.

Dan chooses the easy place and easy way—Laish, a quiet area far to the north and isolated from allies (Judges 18:7). Why fight Philistines when you can blitz Laish? Their love for ease went hand-in-hand with their turning to idols. The five spies did not go to Shiloh to discover the will of God; they went to Micah's shrine and hired a priest (vv. 5, 17–19). They knew what the living God wanted, but they wanted a self-made god who would fit into their lifestyle without making any demands.

It is so tempting to carve out a Laish for ourselves—a quiet little island where we can live in affluence and forget about the needy world outside, the enemies of the gospel, and Jesus' radical claims on our lives. But if we want to live in Laish, we must become idol-worshippers. No consistent New Testament Christian can live a life of ease. No lover of the cross can retire from God's mission in the world. **If we want to settle down into life as comfortable Christians, unconcerned about people's need and God's call, we are going to have to serve an idol.**

What is the outcome of Dan's commitment to easy living? At first, it looks like everything works out beautifully. We see them overwhelming the people of Laish, burning and rebuilding the city, then living a life of ease with their own priesthood and idolatrous shrine (vv. 27–31). However, you don't always reap the harvest of your sins immediately. In 1 Chronicles 4–7, Dan is missing from the list of Israel's tribes and families. They had vanished into obscurity, probably because of intermarriage with the Philistines. In Revelation 7:4–8, Dan is again missing from the list of tribes making up the 144,000 Hebrew believers.

Dan did not take what God had given them, and they took what God had not given them. In the process, they lost all that they had.

Day 49

The book of Judges turns to its last major character, a Levite from Ephraim. Notice that Levites were featured as a central part of the problem in this incident and that of Micah, as if to show the corruption of the religious establishment.

This Levite is an utterly despicable human being. He sacrifices the woman to save himself (Judges 19:25); is able to sleep while she is being abused (19:26); has no thought of her (19:28); and doesn't respect her even in death (19:29). The men of Gibeah are guilty of a horrific evil, but the Levite's call for justice rings hollow.

Israel's gathering of 400,000 men to deal with the injustice (Judges 20:1–2), is also remarkable: the entire nation is drawn together for the first time in Judges, but it is directed against itself. There was never a time in Israel's history when the nation needed God's guidance most desperately, but bloodlust had taken over. Why were the Benjaminites not invited to the assembly (20:3) and asked to take the lead in punishing their fellow tribesmen in Gibeah? Why was no attempt made to find corroborating witnesses (20:4–5)?

Rather than turning to God and seeking His will, Israel does what is right in their own eyes, jumping to military action without attempting judicial negotiation or solutions (Judges 20:8–11). The spirit of revenge pushes for immediate, not measured, response. The tribe of Benjamin, meanwhile, not only refuses to punish the guilty, but are also willing to defend them with their lives (20:13–14).

When the civil war turns against them (Judges 20:21, 25), Israel finally seeks God's direction. But it isn't to ask whether they should go to war; they have already answered that question. Only when 40,000 men lie dead do they deeply seek God's direction (20:26–28) before reducing the tribe of Benjamin to 600 men. Ironically, a people who had refused to carry out holy war against the Canaanites have now carried it out with thoroughness against one of their own tribes.

We live at a time when a thick moral fog has settled upon society. The old moral landmarks have been obliterated, and no one seems to know the difference between right and wrong. It is very tempting to live by our own standards, doing whatever is right in our own eyes. Without God, everything and anything goes. The alternative is to be guided by someone who can see what we cannot see and who knows what we do not know. **The great promise**

of God's Word is that if we commit ourselves to doing what is right in God's eyes, we will be directed safely through the moral fog.

ThinkThrough

How might we be tempted to do things that seem right in our own eyes, without seeking God's guidance?

How can we tell whether an accepted rule or societal norm is in line with God's Word or not?

Read Judges 21:1–25

All of a sudden, the people wake up to the consequences of their bloodlust. They are about to wipe out one of their tribes and leave a gap in the nation. What follows would be comical if it were not so tragic. They have shown no concern for larger issues of truth and justice, but now they show a concern for legalities. They devote enormous ingenuity to finding ways around foolish vows—ways that conform externally to their commitments but mock any ethical instincts.

As usual, God is portrayed as being to blame (Judges 21:3, 15). The implication is that He should have prevented this state of affairs. It is typical of sinful humans to insist on their own way and then blame God for the results.

Yet none of this had to do with idolatry. It began with individuals ignoring the law of God, doing what was right in their own eyes, and it led a whole nation into moral collapse. Israel turned its back on the living God and allowed itself to be overrun by moral relativism, sexual libertinism, and religious syncretism and pluralism.

The slogan "everyone did as he saw fit" (Judges 17:6; 21:25) captures the lifestyle of society today as much as it did then; individualism has been enthroned as the supreme good, and self-fulfilment and self-gratification are its ethics. The basis of moral behaviour is thus critical. If our moral behaviour is not grounded on the absolutes of God's Word, we will end up doing what is right in our own eyes. The only certain basis for morality is the character and Word of God; right and wrong are not what people think they are, but what God says they are.

We also need a personal, dynamic faith in Jesus Christ. We need to make God's values so much a part of us that we instinctively turn to them when moral clarity is impaired. That is why we need fellowship with other Christians whom we can observe and with whom we can honestly discuss our moral struggles.

But if Judges tells of strong men made weak by self-confidence, it also describes weak men and women made strong through faith in God and by His work in their lives; it describes the transforming work of the Spirit. Today, we serve a risen Saviour, live by the power of His indwelling Spirit, and possess the complete Word of God. **Our resources in Christ far outstrip anything the judges knew, and our potential for spiritual victory is far greater than theirs.**

God's strength does not remove human weakness;
it transforms it, so that those with fearful hearts
and feet of clay become people with hearts of iron
to serve their God.

ThinkThrough

What can we do
to become people
with "hearts of iron"
instead of "feet of
clay"?

In the light of the
great resources we
have in Christ, how
can we live up to our
full potential?

Going Deeper
in Your Walk
with Christ

Whether you're a new Christian or have been a Christian for a while, it's worth taking a journey through the gospels of Matthew, Mark, Luke, and John. Each gospel presents a distinct aspect of Christ and helps us gain a deeper appreciation of who Jesus is, why He came, and what it means for us.

Hear His words. Witness His works. Deepen your walk with Jesus as you follow Him through the wonderful scenes painted in the gospels.

JourneyThrough
Matthew
Mike Raiter

JourneyThrough
Mark
Robert M. Solomon

JourneyThrough
Luke
Mike Raiter

JourneyThrough
John
David Cook

Journey Through
Acts

The book of Acts is one of the most exciting parts of the Bible. Jesus has just ascended to heaven, the Spirit has come to the church, and we see God at work building the church and causing the gospel message to spread through Judea, into Samaria, throughout Asia, into Europe, and finally to Rome. Embark on a daily journey through the book of Acts, and see how the Holy Spirit empowers the church to witness in ever widening circles until the gospel reaches the ends of the earth.

David Cook was Principal of the Sydney Missionary and Bible College for 26 years. He is an accomplished writer and has authored Bible commentaries, books on the Minor Prophets, and several Bible study guides.

Journey Through
Hebrews

Have you ever had second thoughts about being a Christian? Sometimes it's hard to stay committed to Jesus amid the daily onslaught of worldly wisdom, tedium, and temptation. Let the book of Hebrews remind you about the Author and Perfecter of our faith; who He is, what He did, and why it matters. Be encouraged by the unique truth of a God who became a man to die in our place and who, as our eternal High Priest, will return bringing eternal rest for those who have anchored their faith in Him.

Robert M. Solomon served as Bishop of The Methodist Church in Singapore from 2000–2012. He has an active itinerant preaching and teaching ministry in Singapore and abroad. He is the author of more than 30 books, including *The Race, The Conscience, The Sermon of Jesus, Faithful to the End, Finding Rest for the Soul,* and *God in Pursuit.*

ABOUT THE PUBLISHER

Discovery House Publishing™
produces a wide array of premium
and quality resources that focus on Scripture,
show reverence for God and His Word,
demonstrate the relevance of vibrant faith,
and equip and encourage you to draw closer
to God in all seasons of your life.

NOTE TO THE READER

We invite you to share your response to the message
of this book by writing to us at:

5 Pereira Road #07-01
Asiawide Industrial Building
Singapore 368025

or sending an email to:

dhpsingapore@dhp.org